THE GAMEKEEPER

The GAMEKEEPER

A Year in the Glen

Charlie Pirie
with Iain Fraser Grigor

Photographs by Charlie Crawford

BBC Books

This book is published to accompany the television series
entitled *The Gamekeeper* which was produced by BBC Scotland
and first broadcast in 1995

Executive producer: Kenneth MacQuarrie
Producer and Director: Stuart Greig
Assistant producer: Sue Hall

Published by BBC Books
an imprint of BBC Worldwide Publishing
BBC Worldwide Limited
Woodlands
80 Wood Lane
London W12 0TT

First published 1995

ISBN 0 563 37177 3

Designed by Tim Higgins
Map by Venture Graphics
Photographs by Charlie Crawford
Set in Monotype Imprint, Modern Extended and Scotch Roman by
Selwood Systems Ltd, Midsomer Norton
Colour separations by Radstock Reproductions Ltd, Midsomer Norton
Printed and bound in Great Britain by Butler & Tanner Ltd, Frome
Jacket printed by Lawrence Allen Ltd, Weston-super-Mare

Contents

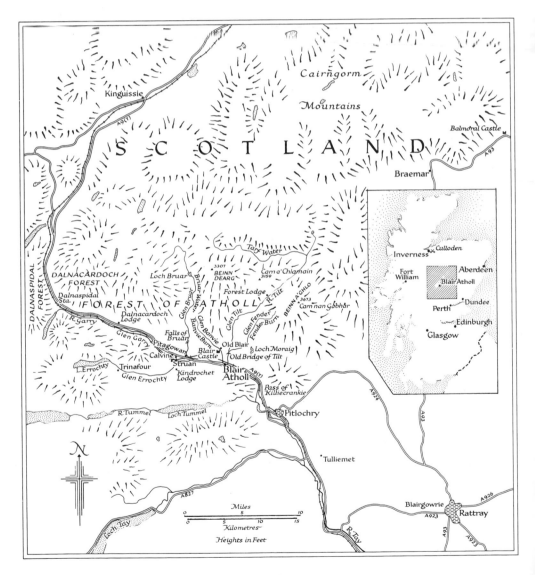

❦ JANUARY ❦

January the first. Hogmanay has come and gone once again, all around the country people have been up half the night, for a good few people maybe the whole night, celebrating, and there are quite a few sore heads around the place, the same as for years and years back, and I am sure for years and years to come. But for us folk here, or at least those of us who are keen on field sports, the big event of New Year's Day is the clay-pigeon shoot, when everyone gets the chance to see how good they are with a shotgun. It's a traditional thing with people who go in for field sports, and it's a fair test of just how good someone is – it really does measure their speed and accuracy with a firearm.

Clay pigeons are small clay targets, a bit like a thick saucer, and they are thrown into the air from a spring-loaded launcher called a trap. If you hit them properly, they disintegrate into small pieces; they're not dangerous for animals because the bits left lying around just waste away with the weather.

Now, there can be two kinds of shooting on New Year's Day. Sometimes I will put on a shoot for my friends, and they like to come along and help out with it. Maybe fifteen or twenty of them come along with their shotguns, and perhaps some of their sons, daughters or wives will turn up as well. Everyone will have a shotgun, maybe twelve-bore or twenty-bore, and there will be someone to load and fire the trap, which could be anywhere – behind a bank, inside some trees or something like that. You can get all different sorts of dispatch with the clays. They can come in slow or fast, high or low, from dead ahead or from the side, even from behind. This sort of shoot is great fun, because the clays fly in a way that is similar to a lot of birds – pigeons, pheasants, partridges and even the hoodie crow.

Celebrating the New Year
at Forest Lodge

New Year's Day: clay-pigeon shooting

Everyone competing will have, say, twenty or twenty-five shots, and whoever hits the largest number of clays is obviously the winner. If there is a tie, then there has to be a shoot-off, and usually you make the guns stand back an extra twenty yards, or else adjust the trap to throw the clays faster than before. Most gamekeepers tend to be roughly the same class of shot – and if there is a bottle of whisky at stake, you may be sure it will be a gamekeeper who steps up to collect it!

The second kind of a New Year's Day shoot can take the form of an instructional day, sometimes for just a few guests and sometimes for as many as a hundred people. They might be guests of the estate, or they might be parties from local hotels. If we have a hundred folk, then we could be talking about going through two thousand cartridges and two thousand clays in one day, so it takes a fair bit of organizing. Some of these people might never have seen a gun before, so the safety aspect is extremely important.

What I do is this: I get a bucket, paint a human face on it, and put it on a post at about eight yards' distance. Then I discharge a shotgun at it, to show people just how destructive a gun can be. I proceed to fire a twelve-bore shotgun directly into the centre of the bucket, and it goes to show all the people who are there, as well as to remind myself, just what terrible damage can be done if a shotgun is used in the wrong manner. And when a face is painted on the bucket it really gets home to people – it puts an extra wee thought in their mind to be very, very careful with a weapon like that.

But instead of talking about shooting – even though it is a big passion for me – I had better introduce myself, tell you something about my own background and how I came to be the gamekeeper at Forest Lodge on the Atholl estate in Perthshire, living with my family eight miles or so up one of the remotest glens in Scotland, and surrounded by some of the wildest wildlife in the country: deer, grouse, foxes, mountain hares and golden eagles.

I suppose you could say it all started thirty-odd years ago, when as a lad of fifteen I got my first job with the estate – not up here in the wilds of Glen Tilt, but down at Tulliemet, about fifteen miles south of Blair Atholl on the Perth road. It is a nice area and was a great place for a young lad to start off his working life at, because you had everything in the gamekeeping world – grouse, pheasants, partridges and most of the other gamebirds too. There was a nice stretch of salmon river. You had two very nice lochs, some excellent roe-deer and fallow-deer stalking, and during the shooting season the chance to act as pony-man.

A couple or so years after that I was very lucky because I was asked to be an assistant stalker. That doesn't come the way of every seventeen-year-old, and I have stalked more or less every year since then. But after another two years I got married to my wife Sandra. We were married very quietly back in Kirriemuir by my old minister, who had given me a reference to come to the job. It was nice for him to see me back getting married after having written out a reference for employment on the estate.

So after that we left Tulliemet and moved to Kindrochit, a few miles west of Blair Atholl, where Glen Errochty meets Glen Garry at Struan.

This was a great place to start off married life, and there was no shortage of work to be getting on with. The amount of deer there depended on the weather. Some years you would be lucky to get ten hinds, and in other years you could easily be shooting fifty beasts. It was a very good area for roe-deer too, and that was another crop we took off. And of course there was a small amount of grouse and pheasants – some years we would put down two hundred, and in other years as many as five hundred.

When I started there, the partridge situation was very good, but it has gone a long way downhill since then – a combination, I suppose, of weather and predators and the effect of new methods of farming, which leave less and less food for the birds.

Anyway, we stayed at Kindrochit, myself and the family, for twenty-odd years, until one day I got a call from the factor, and he said with great deliberation that the duke himself had decided that I was to go to Forest Lodge as the head stalker. Well, I was very excited at that – but I wanted to know about the stalker who was there at the time; he was a friend of mine, you see. But he was getting older, and it is a hard part of the country to work. So eventually it was decided that he would come down and I would go up. If you like, we swapped positions – and that's how I came to Glen Tilt. In a way, mind you, I was sorry to be leaving, because we had been there so long, the kids had grown up there, Sandra had her job, there was a good school with a good teacher, and there was a lot of friendship in the community. It was a very close community and great fun to be part of.

We moved up to Forest Lodge in the summer of 1992, over a period of two or three weeks. It was quite a thing to do, a flitting of a whole family up the Glen Tilt road – it must be one of the most dangerous in Scotland, though it's not so bad in the summer. But it's not a road you want to go off in the wintertime, that's for sure! But for me in particular this flitting was at an exciting time. It was July when we moved, and the grouse season was about ready to start, and I had to get out there and find out the names of all the hills and burns and so on.

I suppose you could say that coming to Forest Lodge was the crown of my ambition. I had always wanted to be a gamekeeper, and this must be one of the best gamekeeping jobs in the whole of Scotland. For as long as I can remember, this was the job for me. My mother tells me that from the age of two or three I was

interested in guns and game and things like that. My father died
when I was twelve, and I owe a lot to my mother. She brought me
up after that, and I will always remember what a help her enthusi-
asm and support have been over the years. I suppose I maybe
inherited this love of the countryside from my father, who was also
a gamekeeper, and he loved the job too. I got an airgun when I was
maybe six years of age, and I can remember being told that I
would be shooting at pigeons and so forth about that age.

Mind you, it didn't take long to discover that a gamekeeper
wasn't a shooting machine – you had a hell of a lot of hard work to
put in before you actually used a gun or a rifle as a keeper. I wasn't
long in my first job before this became very obvious. In those days
it wasn't a five-day week and then 'knock off at three o'clock on a
Friday' sort of attitude, like the young lads nowadays seem to
think. Or some of them anyway – keener on getting away down to
the disco instead of getting on with the work that needs to be done.
Not all of them, mind, but some of them.

Maybe, of course, being brought up to it, and having a natural
liking for it, made things fairly easy for me. I had been going to
local clay-pigeon shoots since I was eight; I was in competition
teams and winning prizes by the age of ten. And by the time I was
twelve I would be at hare-shoots – you know, taking time off school
sometimes, and going to shoots every Saturday morning right
through the winter. So I had shot hundreds and hundreds of hares
and crows and pigeons long before I ever started out working at
the job.

It wasn't as if I didn't know what the job involved, because I
had been mixing with what you might call the professionals from
a very early age. Indeed, it was when I was thirteen that I got my
first gun. I had to work six weeks of my summer holidays to get
this twelve-bore BSA shotgun. I can still remember paying the 10
shillings – that's 50p nowadays – to get the licence for it. I can
tell you this, there weren't many guns in Scotland looked after
better than that one was! And by the time I was fourteen I was
winning a lot of competitions with that gun as far away as places
like Montrose and so on.

So we have been up here in Glen Tilt since 1992, and though
the day-to-day work is pretty much in my own hands, obviously

it's the estate that shapes the strategy of what goes on. The Atholl estate is a very well-managed one in my opinion, and I must say it has always been lucky with the sort of factors it has had. Sometimes there are wee disagreements – that's just natural – but of course the factor maybe knows something I don't know about. But more or less always we are given our head, meaning that if we say something in the game-shooting department, they usually listen and nearly always agree with us.

And on Atholl the factor is never on our backs all the time like he is on some other estates. Some factors, some owners, are never off their keepers' backs, you know, but not here. A lot of things are left to our own discretion on Atholl. Of course, it works both ways. We are well aware of the economic side of things and try to keep estate costs down; the less money you put out, the better it is for the estate. For example, we will run the tractor tyres until they are really finished and absolutely have to be changed – there are lots of other examples like that. Basically, it comes down to not wasting money – and in the long run, that means the duke's money.

I have great respect for the duke; he is a very shy man, but he likes his field sports. It is obviously him that keeps us all in a job here, and most people have worked for him for a long time. Sometimes the duke comes up to Forest Lodge, and sometimes we go down and assist him at the shoots, when he has guests and so on. He allows the estate to be used by a lot of folk who don't live on it: horse-trials, for instance, camping facilities to the likes of Boy Scouts, car rallies and archery championships. There is also a horrific amount of hill-walkers, thousands and thousands of them, who come on to his ground.

He has never said, once, to them to get off the ground, though maybe sometimes keepers and factors have asked walkers to do such and such a thing during the shooting season. I am sure the duke has his own ideas, but he has never once said to walkers what and what not to do. In the past, of course, some of the dukes have, and they have been taken to task for it and it has made publicity – but that has never happened with the present duke.

In a way I suppose you could say that the estate is a bit like a family on an extended scale – on a lot bigger scale compared to a family like my own. Once we were married, Isla came along after a year or so, and then there was Bob – his real name is Charles, but everyone calls him Bob, after Fat Bob in Oor Wullie in the *Sunday Post*. Number three was Mark, two years after Bob, and Carol is the last of them. Isla is twenty-two and working in Stornoway. It is a long way off, Stornoway; there is the Minch to cross and ferries and what have you, but she comes down every now and again, and sometimes we go out to Lewis and see her.

Bob is next, he has just turned twenty-one and is a trainee gamekeeper with the estate. He has done it since he left school, and loves the job. Indeed, he is very lucky to have it. Jobs for gamekeepers these days are few and far between. It is very difficult to get a job. I mean, you go for an interview and there is even a short-leet from maybe three hundred applicants, and some of them are postmen, bankers, joiners, anything at all except gamekeepers.

Mark is number-two son and third in the family. He is twenty. He works on the estate too – he just went down to the factor and asked if he could get a job, though I didn't know about it at the time. He went to college and did the same YTS courses as Bob did.

They all excel at something. Bob is a very good deer-stalker, and Mark is terrific at controlling the foxes. He has come out with me since he was five or six, and can find foxes where even foxhounds can't find them.

Carol is the youngest; she has just turned eighteen. She was very lucky; she had just left school but got a job in the hotel, and she likes the work there. She hoped to be a nanny – she is very good with children – but people can't afford nannies too much these days, so she was lucky with the hotel. I mean, let's be fair, work is limited in this area; there are only a few sorts of jobs on offer. She does still like the idea of working with children, but we can't have everything, and we should all be grateful to have a job. She likes to do a wee bit of the disco-dancing, but otherwise is quite sensible – in fact, all four of them are pretty sensible.

As for their future here – well, no one can see too far into the

RIGHT *Walking home through the snow with pheasants*

BELOW *Charlie's son Mark on a pheasant shoot*

Returning to the vehicles at the end of the day's shoot

future these days, whether for ourselves, for the children, or even the estate itself.

I would like to think that things would continue pretty much as they always have. But then there are changes everywhere, and this district is no different. Even in gamekeeping I have seen big changes; hopefully, there will always be work for a keeper, but I think things will be done in other ways. There will be more and more restrictions on what can be done and what can't be done. That will mean less work around – for keepers, for the people in the estate office, for the blacksmith who shoes the ponies, for the local shops or whoever.

The day might come when guests no longer come to shoot the deer. Maybe then the job of the keeper will be all conservation, and that might mean one man replacing the five men needed at the moment. Grouse-shooting could come under pressure too – not least because of changes in the natural environment, never mind the law! And if the sheep go – well, the shepherd will have to go too, and his cottage will become maybe a holiday home for a few weeks in the summer, and all you will have in Glen Tilt will be a bit of walking and a bit of sightseeing.

This is the way things seem to be going just now. I hope it doesn't come for a long time ... I hope it doesn't come in my lifetime. But we just don't know, nobody knows nowadays. The future is uncertain. It would be fine and grand if we could carry on the way we were, though I don't see it happening.

But even if things do change – well, the countryside is still there to be looked after, and it always will be. I always wanted to be a gamekeeper, and am tremendously lucky that that is what I have done. It is a fantastic job. I really think it is the best job in the whole world, and it still will be, whatever the future might hold.

By Dog, Dirk and Dagger

Glen Tilt has for centuries been the greatest of the Scottish deer-grounds and has in its time been witness to many different forms of hunting (and not only for deer, as wolves were once common in the Scottish countryside).

Today, of course, and for at least a century and a half past, the established method of hunting has been stalking, which involves a relatively small party (or sole hunter) working its way slowly across difficult ground until the chosen beast is brought within range of a powerful rifle.

But in earlier ages, before the development of reliable firearms, other means were necessary. Of these, there were three principal forms, none of which, at least legally, is now practised in the Highlands.

The first was baiting, by which specially selected dogs would drive herds of deer (taking care not to panic them) on to a pre-positioned party of hunters.

The second – coursing – involved sighting deer in the distance, closing in as closely as possible, and then 'slipping' (unleashing) powerful and magnificent hounds, which would chase and kill one or more of the deer (or themselves be killed in the attempt).

The third – driving – was on a much greater scale, with the prey herded on to the waiting hunters (in the manner of a modern grouse-shoot). This form involved huge numbers of beaters, who, over days, would enclose a vast number of deer and drive them towards the hunters. The hunters would then slaughter as many beasts as they could, with whatever means were to hand – 'dogs, guns, arrows, dirks and daggers', according to John Taylor, the 'Thames water-poet', as he was known.

In Scotland these great deer-drives were known as tinchels and, over the centuries, have been described in some detail by a number of observers.

According to the Stuarts in *Lays of the Deer Forest*:

> *The tinchel, or greater driving, is now entirely disused in Scot-*
> *land, though it was a mode of hunting common to all countries*
> *from a high antiquity. Even in our own time, in Hungary,*
> *Bohemia, the Thuringian Forest, and some other German prin-*
> *cipalities, the* grandes battues *sometimes exhibit a feudal*

21

By Dog, Dirk and Dagger

magnificence and armies of retainers, which recall the splendid forest-gatherings of the Middle Ages.

In 1822 the late Prince Esterhazy held at Ozora a battue, *the drivers of which amounted to four thousand men, by whom during a day and a night the game of a great tract of wooded country were driven into the central forests; and in the six days of shooting which followed in this area, there were killed ten hundred and eighty-seven head, including deer, wild boars, wolves, foxes and hares.*

The tinchel of Scotland was exactly similar in spirit and organization to these continental extravaganzas – '*the highest and most passionate enjoyment of hunting in the Highlands*'.

Of such a tinchel, the Stuarts write:

It was performed by enclosing a large extent of ground within a circular cordon of beaters, who drove the deer into one glen or wood, the passes of which were guarded by bows, guns and dogs. In the great gatherings, particularly for the 'Royal Huntings', several hundred men were employed, sometimes for two or three weeks, and whole districts were surrounded, and the game driven into an appointed tryst.

The most remarkable of these great huntings known to us were those given by the Earl of Atholl to King James v and Queen Mary. The first of these was accompanied by that extraordinary and lavish magnificence, which frequently demonstrates that the descriptions and manners of the Romances of Chivalry were drawn from the real life of the Middle Ages.

We can thank the Scottish historian Lindsay of Pitscottie for his

---

The huntsmen were armed with swords and daggers, and sometimes with bows and arrows; but the main agents of destruction were the dogs. For centuries pursuit by dogs was the essence of the chase; other means of taking deer, such as girnes [snares], nets and crossbows, were considered unsporting, and forbidden by law; and firearms, when they became available, excited particular disapproval.

Duff Hart-Davis, *Monarchs of the Glen*

By Dog, Dirk and Dagger

> ❧ *The climax of each drive must have been*
> *barbaric in the extreme – a frenzy of slaughter.*
> *At one tinchel, it is recorded, John Robertson of Easter*
> *Tyre and John Stewart of Blair Atholl each cut a stag*
> *clean in half with a single blow of his broadsword.*
>
> Duff Hart-Davis, *Monarchs of the Glen*

description of the first of these: the great tinchel of 1528, for which the earl had an ambitious hunting-lodge specially constructed.

According to Lindsay,

> *The Earl of Atholl, hearing of the king's coming, made great provision for him in all things pertaining to a prince, that he was as well served and eased with all things necessary to his estate, as he had been in his own palace of Edinburgh. For I heard say, this noble earl caused to be built a curious palace for the king, his mother, and the ambassador, where they were as honourably eased and lodged as they had been in England, France, Italy, or Spain, concerning the time and the equivalent for their hunting and pastime, which was built in the middle of a fair meadow.*
>
> *Its walls were of green timber, woven with green birches, fashioned four-square, and in each corner there was a tower, as if the building were a fort, three storeys high. The floors were covered with rushes, reeds and flowers, that no man knew where he was, but as he had been in a garden. There were also two towers on each side of the entrance-gate, which was furnished with a wooden portcullis, a drawbridge, and a moat sixteen feet deep and thirty feet wide.*
>
> *And also this palace within was hung with fine tapestry and silken screens, and lit with fine glass windows; this palace was as pleasantly decorated with all necessaries pertaining to a prince as it had been his own palace royal at home. The halls and chambers were prepared with costly bedding, vessels and napery, according for a king, who remained in this wilderness at the hunting the space of three days and three nights.*

Adds Lindsay, with characteristic attention to detail: '*I have heard men say it cost the Earl of Atholl every day in expenses £1000*'.

Curiously, Lindsay did not bother to record any detail of the hunt, or

23

By Dog, Dirk and Dagger

> 🌿 *Up to the eighteenth century great formal hunts were periodically organized by the Highland nobles and lairds, and one of the dues owed by most Highland tenants was to attend at their superior's hunting. The place to which the game – wolves and foxes as well as deer – were driven was known as the 'Elrick', and this is a common place-name in the Highlands.*
>
> I. F. Grant, *Highland Folk Ways*

of the total number of deer and other game which were killed – but the bag must have been immense.

Certainly, the tinchel was long remembered in the area. Almost 250 years later, during the course of his tour of Scotland, the writer Thomas Pennant visited the Forest of Atholl and found, at a narrow and difficult part of it, a rock known as the King's Seat, a point from which King James must have directed the great three-day hunt.

And in 1563, John, fourth Earl of Atholl, hosted a tinchel for Queen Mary, one of whose courtiers, William Barclay, left an eye-witness account:

> *Two thousand Highlanders were employed to drive to the hunting-ground all the deer from the woods and hills of Atholl, Badenoch, Mar, Moray and the countries about. As these Highlanders are used to light dress, and are very swift of foot, they brought together two thousand red deer, besides roe- and fallow-deer. The queen, the great men, and a number of others, were in a glen when all these deer were brought before them. The whole body of deer moved forward like an order of battle, and they had a leader whom they followed wherever he moved.*
>
> *This leader was a very fine stag, with a very high head. This sight delighted the queen very much, but she soon had cause for fear, upon the earl saying – 'There is danger in that stag, for if either fear or rage force him from the ridge of the hill, let each look to himself, for none will be out of harm's way, for the rest will all follow him and having thrown us under foot will open their passage to the hill behind us'.*
>
> *What happened a moment after confirmed this opinion; for the queen ordered one of the best dogs to be let loose on one of the deer; this the dog pursues, the leading stag was frightened, he*

By Dog, Dirk and Dagger

flies by the same way that he came, the rest rush after him, and break out through the thickest body of Highlanders. They had nothing for it but to throw themselves flat on the heath, and to allow the deer to pass over them. It was told the queen that several of the Highlanders had been wounded, and that two or three were killed on the spot; and the whole body had got off, had not the Highlanders, by their skill in hunting, fallen upon a stratagem to cut off the rear from the main body. It was of those which had been separated that the queen's dogs and those of the nobility made slaughter. There were killed that day three hundred and sixty deer, five wolves, and some roes.

Even when royalty was absent, the tinchels were still on an enormous scale. John Taylor attended one in the early seventeenth century, and also left an eye-witness account:

Being arrived at the tryst, there did I find the truly noble and right honourable lords, John Erskine, Earl of Mar; James Stuart, Earl of Murray; George Gordon, Earl of Enzie, son and heir to the Marquis of Huntley; James Erskine, Earl of Buchan; and Lord John Erskine, son and heir to the Earl of Mar, and their Countesses; with my much honoured, and my last assured and approved friend, Sir William Murray, Knight, of Abercairney; and hundreds of others, knights, esquires, and their followers; all and every man in general in one habit; for once in a year,

> *In the late nineteenth century, deer-forest owners were asked about the extent to which they still used hounds. The answers indicate the extent to which they had more or less disappeared from hunting.*
> *Brechin – 'We generally find the collie more useful than the staghound, as the latter will not follow a track, but runs only by sight, while a good collie will follow the track of a wounded stag through fresh deer.'*
> *Ross-shire – 'I consider a good collie as far superior to any other kind of dog for a wounded deer.'*
> *Kinlochmore – 'We occasionally use collie dogs as trackers for wounded deer; and for tracking deer I think no dog so good as a good collie.'*
> E. W. Bell, *The Scottish Deerhound*

By Dog, Dirk and Dagger

which is the whole month of August and sometimes part of September, many of the nobility and gentry of the kingdom do come into these Highland countries to hunt, where they do conform themselves to the habits of the Highlanders.

The manner of the hunting is this. Five or six hundred men do rise early in the morning, and they do disperse themselves divers ways; and seven, eight or ten miles compass, they do bring or chase in the deer in many herds, two, three, or four hundred in a herd, to such or such a place as the noblemen shall appoint them; then, when day is come, the lords and gentlemen of their companies do ride or go to the said places, sometimes wading up to the middle through burns and rivers; and then they, being come to the place, do lie down on the ground, till those foresaid scouts, which are called the 'Tinkhell', do bring down the deer; but as the proverb says of a bad cook, so these tinkhell men do lick their own fingers; for besides their bows and arrows which they carry with them, we can hear now and then a arquebuss or a musket go off, which they do seldom discharge in vain.

Then, after we had stayed there three hours or thereabouts, we might perceive the deer appear on the hills round about us, their heads making a show like a wood, which being followed close by the tinkhell, are chased down into the valley where we lay; then

---

The Duke of Atholl's estate is very extensive, and the country populous; while vassalage existed, the chieftain could raise two or three thousand fighting men, and leave sufficient at home to take care of the ground. The forests, or rather chases (for they are quite naked), are very extensive, and feed vast numbers of Stags, which range, at certain times of the year, in herds of five hundred. Some grow to a great size: I have heard of one that weighed 18 stone, Scots, or 314 pounds exclusive of head, entrails and skin. The hunting of these animals was formerly after the manner of an Eastern monarch. Thousands of vassals surrounded a great tract of country, and drove the Deer to the spot where the Chieftains were stationed, who shot them at their leisure.

Thomas Pennant, *Tour in Scotland*, 1771

By Dog, Dirk and Dagger

all the valley on each side being waylaid with a hundred couple of strong Irish greyhounds, they are all let loose, as occasion serves, upon the herd of deer; that with dogs, guns, arrows, dirks and daggers, in the space of two hours four-score fat deer were slain; which after were disposed of some one way, and some another, twenty and thirty miles, and more than enough left for us to make merry withal at our rendezvous.

That hunt was in 1618, and the tinchel remained the principal form of hunting for another couple of centuries.

In 1655, for instance, the Earl of Seaforth hosted a tinchel at Monar for the Master and Tutor of Lovat and his brother, Hugh Fraser of Struy: a relatively small-scale affair, with just a hundred retainers to support the gentlemen of the party.

The Tutor pitched his tent on the north side of the river and Struy his tent upon the south. Next day we got sight of six or seven hundred deer, and sport of hunting fitter for kings than country gentlemen. The four days we tarried there, what is it that could cheer and renovate men's spirits but was gone about? – jumping, shooting, throwing the bar, the stone, and all manner of manly exercises imaginable; and for entertainment, our baggage was well furnished of beef, mutton, fowls, fishes, fat venison, a very princely camp, and all manner of liquors. Masters Hill and Man, two Englishmen who were in the company, declared that in all their travels they never had such brave divertisement.

And 150 years later, hunting in the old way was still being pursued at Atholl. In 1800 the fourth duke's daughter wrote to her brother, *'Papa had a famous deer-hunt yesterday; there were above 200 tenants there, who formed a line four miles in length. They surrounded about twelve hundred deer, but they broke through their line and got off, so that they only killed six of them.'*

But by now the days of the tinchel were numbered. And with it went the days of the magnificent staghound (against which animosity, on account of the savage use to which it was put, is surely misdirected).

Big dogs, certainly, would remain part of the deer-hunting scene well into the coming century – they appear in many of Landseer's paintings – but as little more than tracker accessories to hunters armed increasingly with better and better rifles.

The day of the nineteenth-century stalker was about to dawn: and though it was a slow dawn, it was no less sure for that.

❧ FEBRUARY ❧

Now this one is the hard month – February, as tough as any of the rest in the year, and sometimes tougher than a few of them put together! The days have stretched a bit but they are still very short, the frosts are bitter, times are desperate for the animals on the hill, and above all else there is the snow. At times there is so much of it that you would think we spent ninety per cent of our working day battling against it. Pretty much all ways, it is a savage sort of month – for the sheep, for the deer – and hard enough too for the people who live in the glen and work in it: when the snow will let them work.

Just about always, February is a bad month for weather – though of course some are even worse than the usual. The trouble is, you never really can tell when you're going to get a bad one, though there are those who say you can spot the signs back in the autumn.

Some people would say the berries will give a warning. If you see a lot of berries on the trees, then you will get such-and-such a kind of winter, though I think myself it's a bit of an old wives' tale. A lot of berries is supposed to be a warning that a bad winter is on the way. Back in the autumn you see the rowan berries and rosehips and that sort of thing – and often enough you will see the birds going at them if there's not much else for them to eat – from about November onwards, though I have seen them myself a few weeks earlier. That's supposed to be another sign – the birds eating the berries even though they are very bitter. It's supposed to be a sign that the birds know a bad winter is on the way. Another one is the deer coming down from the hill early, or a lot of flowers growing at the side of the road.

But I am not convinced myself. I have seen winters in this area when the snow-drifts were up over the top of the house, and you can only think to yourself, 'Well, that's funny now, I could swear there weren't many berries around last autumn.'

Take the early eighties as an example. The last really bad winter we had here was in 1980–81. We had frost at the end of October, and then snow at the end of November – and we had it right through for three months without a break. We were going from the house to the burn every morning, because the waterpipes were frozen solid. We would go to the burn and chip our way through the ice to get a bucket filled. In fact we were using that water all through the winter – boiling it for drinking for two and a half months non-stop.

And I can't remember seeing any signs the previous autumn either. That winter just seemed to have come out of nowhere. And anyway, signs or not, we still get the frosts and the snows, and we just have to live with them, whether we had early warnings or not. We just have to keep going, whatever the weather throws at us, because this is where we live, and this is where we work.

Sometimes it is so cold that there is trouble with transport. That happened a lot back in the early eighties, and especially in that winter of 1980–81. Diesel fuel was freezing up in a lot of tanks, but I had a jeep with a winch on the front and it used petrol so that kept running. And we fitted a snow-plough to the front of an old tractor, which was a big help in keeping the roads passable. Every morning at six I was out with the plough so that the nurse could get out to visit a sick patient. Normally, of course, the council would have done it, but they didn't have the resources. And you can understand that – even the A9 was blocked for a full three weeks and there was next to nothing going up on the railway either.

Our little community here was blocked in, and it's at times like those that people just have to muck in and help each other out. Otherwise I don't know that you would have anyone living in a place like this.

When the snow is bad, we just have to keep going and be prepared for anything – snow or not, there is always something of one kind or another to be attended to. So if we get a really good day of hard-packed crispy snow, we could have someone away down the glen to get fuel because obviously we only keep so much

RIGHT *A snow-ploughed track leading to Forest Lodge*

BELOW *Bruce, the gamekeeper's assistant, working on the snow plough*

of it up the glen. Or we could be cut off with the power down, and that has to be fixed as quickly as possible.

Wet snow, frozen snow, can bring the poles down, so we have to have the generator ready to go at a moment's notice. Or there might be a bit of welding to be done – hard weather is always tough on the machinery, and we are always breaking bits off the snow-plough, for example. Or there might be a vehicle to dig out of a drift – up at Forest Lodge, you can't just phone the AA or the RAC. Well, you could, but they would just tell you to stay where you were, of course!

The great secret is never to panic. I have seen myself getting agitated when tourists go up the glen when they were warned not to. I mean, it's miles up here, and some bits are very bad for snow; and if you go over the side at the wrong place, well, there's nothing there but a drop of two or three hundred feet.

Some of the tourists will tell you 'It's all right, I have a four-wheel-drive vehicle', and maybe they do – but it doesn't mean they know how to drive the thing! So up they go, and they get stuck. That annoys me, to think that we have to live there and fight our way in and out – and these people just drive up, get stuck, and abandon their vehicle, right in the middle of the road, in a snow-drift. And when you talk to them about it, you would think it was your fault – 'The road should have been cleared for me, and you should have provided a bigger lay-by for me', and that sort of attitude.

What you must always be cautious about is when conditions are really bad. I don't mean just a snowstorm, but a real blizzard, when you can't see, you can hardly even breathe. Basically, the snow blows up your nose and you can't do anything about it. It's blowing so hard, it's like pinpricks in your eyes, in your ears … it's up your nose, it's in your mouth – it gets everywhere. There could be a guy standing next to you and even if you shout at him he can't hear a word. Very, very few people have seen conditions as bad as that, but up at Forest Lodge you can get serious blizzards any time during a bad winter.

It's in these conditions that you need the very best of gear in the way of protective clothing, of course. And as important a part of that as any is what you have on your feet, whether good

ABOVE *A Highland cow in Glen Fender*

OPPOSITE *Red deer in winter in Glen Tilt*

PRECEDING PAGE *Charlie Pirie on top of his Land-Rover*

OVERLEAF *The road through the grouse moor in winter*

Collecting a dead pheasant during the shoot

*The day's bag of pheasants
laid out in the snow*

OVERLEAF *View of Loch Moraig*

mountain-shoes or -boots or some sort of waterproof knee-boots.

Now, some people still wear the old style of hill-shoe: basically a hobnail or commando sole, with a very rugged flap out over the laces. Some people love them in the hill in the summer, though obviously they are not much use in wintertime, especially in the sort of snow conditions I have been describing.

But I know keepers who wear nothing else but that sort of shoe. I suppose it's all a matter of preference and each to their own and so on.

But the shoes cost about the same as a pair of good boots, and my preference is for boots any time. Lots of people have different opinions on the precise kind to wear, but I think the safest thing to say is that they should be leather, with some sort of waterproof lining. Twenty-five years ago, of course, you just had horse-hide leather with hobnailed soles, and it didn't matter what you coated them with: you usually ended the day with your feet wet.

But nowadays there is a wide range available, and they are much improved on the old sort of boot. Whatever you choose, it must be a good fit around the ankle. This is very important. The ankle must be properly supported, or some day you will end up in trouble. The same goes for the sole too, naturally. You can have the boots going up your leg a bit – say, a nine-inch upper with eyeholes for the laces. I amn't too keen on hooks for laces as they tend to get caught on various things.

There are lots to choose from, really. The British army boot is one I have a lot of time for, though unfortunately they are not very waterproof. Price has a lot to do with it; it's really up to the individual pocket. You can get a good boot for £100, but you can get a better one for £200. You should always try to get a boot that is best suited to the ground it will be used on. Some soles are useless on high, rough ground but fine for low ground, whereas the boot I am using at the moment has a very good commando sole and is extremely long-lasting.

The heel is another part of the boot which is important. You can get a completely flat sole, with the instep built up inside the boot. To me, that is like a sledge on a slippery ground, whether snow or ice, though a lot of people would not agree. But I like my boots to grip the ground.

Laces might not seem important in the town, but, believe me, they are very important indeed if you are deep into the hills. If you break a lace, say stepping through a bog, then you could lose your boot – lose it for good. And you still have miles of rough mountain and perhaps deep snow to cross before you get home! Just one other thing on boots: when you buy them, make sure that they have a stitched-in tongue, which will make the boot almost completely waterproof.

So that's the sort of hill-boot I would go for. They don't have to be terribly expensive – it's up to your pocket – but I would still say it is worth hanging on for that extra few weeks to be able to buy something up-market in the boot line.

But perhaps the most important thing of all is that boots must be looked after, or they won't last. With leather hill-boots, obviously you need two pairs. You don't really have to clean nylon laces, but you must clean the boots. Take five minutes with an old scrubbing-brush along the seams, the sides, sometimes the soles. If the leather isn't clean before it is dried, the mud will cake and hold water, and won't take wax. There are five or six types of boot-wax. I look after mine with mink wax: it keeps the boots waterproof and supple for a long time. It is best put on with the fingers rather than brushes. You mustn't dry them at an open fire – or, if you have to, then fill them with newspapers and make sure they are at least three feet back from the flames. If you don't, over time the leather will become brittle and will break. But if you do look after them, clean them and wax them and dry them carefully, you'll get years of reliable service from them.

Every keeper also needs a few pairs of rubber boots, naturally, and there are a few kinds on the market, of various prices. The top of the range are leather-lined with a zip up the side. Excellent boots, very comfortable, very warm, easy to get on and off, with a good gripping sole in snow and mud. But they are expensive, whereas your standard green welly shooting-boot is about half the price. That's basically a very good hunter-boot, with buckles on the side, and a good grip. You can get them with a lining which keeps the feet warm, and they usually last for two or three shooting seasons. That's the sort of boot I would recommend people to go for – and they are perfectly good enough for heavy winter conditions as well.

Of course, some people still prefer the leather mountain-boot, even when the weather is really bad – and that's when the snow-gaiter comes into its own. They must have a good, strong nylon zip at the back of the leg – not up the side, but at the back. And they mustn't have too tight a tie at the top. I don't like elasticated tops and bottoms because they slack off after a while, and the snow can get in. Old-style lacings are better. With a good gaiter in snow, whatever you pay for them, they are worth it.

The snow-gaiters are particularly valuable in heavy drifting conditions, and you can get drifts building up very quickly in Glen Tilt. You can have a five-foot drift appear in minutes, and if your vehicle gets stuck in that sort of thing, you must be prepared to spend the night there if conditions are too dangerous to walk. You must keep calm and assess the situation, because if a blizzard is howling then you will be able to see absolutely nothing at all.

Remember, they can last for twenty-four hours, and if you get stuck at dusk it can be very frightening, psychologically it really gets to you. If you can't reverse your way out of it, you can walk back to the nearest house and phone home, let people know what the situation is. But otherwise you are there for the night – which is why you should always carry food, a flask of tea, a sleeping-bag and so on, as well as enough fuel to keep the engine running all night, for the heater.

I have been badly caught out myself once, but that was years and years ago. It wasn't long after I had passed my driving test. It was a Saturday night, I had a mini-van, and I was drummer in a dance band at the time. Well, I was heading for that dance, the snow was really heavy, and I came round a corner and ran straight into a huge snow-drift. There was no way I was getting through it, or out of it, but I just managed to sneak the car off the road a bit, into a gateway.

You can see the way I was thinking – if I sit here in the middle of the road, the snow-plough will come along in the morning and go right over the top of me, he'll never see my wee mini-van covered with snow.

A road beyond Forest Lodge

I wasn't too badly off. I had warm clothes, waterproofs, a sleeping-bag. . . . In fact, I had a half-bottle of Grouse too – the breathalyser wasn't so popular then, so that shows you how long ago it was!

It was a desperate night for weather, mind you. When you stepped outside, even just for a quick stretch, the snow was in your nose, in your eyes, in your ears, everywhere. And the wind – it just sucked the breath out of you. And when I jumped back into the car, there was as much snow inside as out – it just blasted its way in.

So anyway, I fell asleep at last, and about three in the morning I saw lights. I didn't believe it at first, but they were definitely lights – a police Land-Rover. There was a sergeant in charge. He said he knew there would be people stranded, and he had a good idea where to find them, because he could work out from the direction of the wind where there would be bad drifting. So that was one dance I never played at. I got to the place where it was to be, all right, but it was seven in the morning by then.

Mind you, if the weather is hard for us, it can be a lot harder for the sheep – an awful lot harder. In the winter you try to get them down into the woods, into a bit of shelter, but of course there's no guarantee that they will stay there. But they still have to be fed – usually two or three bales of hay every day. Sometimes you have to find them first, and if there has been more snow overnight, and the wind is from a particular direction, then you need to fight through drifts that could be eight foot high.

And of course by this time the ewes are well in lamb, and they have to be looked after or they will just lose the lambs. They have to be fed, and kept clear of the sort of conditions that are really bad for them: wet snow and a hard wind.

In fact, I can remember one man here, he spent a fortnight looking for his sheep after very heavy snow. And when he finally found them some were dead, but some were still alive. After a fortnight, we found them in an air-pocket inside about five feet of snow, beside a wall where they had taken shelter. It wasn't easy finding them – just prod your way along the wall with a stick and hope for the best. We found a lot of them that way, but we were very, very lucky – though it helped a lot that we had a good idea where they were. That guy used to feed his sheep every day inside that wall, and obviously there was a good chance that that was the spot they would take shelter in, waiting for him to come in the morning with something to eat for them.

But the main secret is – be ready for the winter. I am using studs on my tyres now. Last year I was the only vehicle comfortably driving up and down the road. It was a complete sheet of glass from Blair Atholl to Forest Lodge and everyone was going round in circles. Everyone was dead scared to drive – but you have to go up and down, it's as simple as that. We sanded the road at least three times from top to bottom and the next day you would go out and it would have frozen overnight – back to square one.

So from now on it's studs in winter, though they come off some time in the spring, of course. And by the end of February there's always a feeling that the spring isn't so far away, that the end of the winter is in sight at last.

That always cheers people up a bit, I think. The days are stretching at last; you know the winter can't last for ever. I know there's always a bit of excitement at the start of it, but after a while you do get fed up with it. You do get fed up with having to go out and dig snow all the time, of having continually to fight your way through snow-drifts and come up the road like you were driving on a skating-rink.

And the winter is hard on the birds and animals too, all of them, whether deer or sheep or whatever.

So when the spring comes – when March comes round again – you hope it will be a good one, and anyway you are always pleased to see it again. The flowers will be coming out sooner or later, you hear drips of water everywhere and you know the ice is melting – that's when you know that the spring is on its way once more. And it's welcome. Believe me, after a hard winter in Glen Tilt, the spring is more than welcome.

Jacobite Atholl: the '45

The two hundred and fiftieth anniversary of the 1745 Jacobite rising falls in 1995. The following year witnesses the anniversary of the final defeat of that same Jacobite cause at Culloden, outside Inverness, in April 1746. The rising was one in which Atholl men and women of all ranks played a prominent part, as indeed they had in earlier attempts to claim the throne in the name of the exiled James II, and the son who styled himself James III.

Given the long involvement of the earls of Atholl in national affairs, and their intimate connection with the old royalty of Scotland, none of this is surprising. Indeed, the earls and their followers had played a role in Scottish affairs and in Anglo-Scottish relations for five centuries.

They had gone to war against the English in 1296, as a result of which the earl was captured and kept in the Tower of London. Ten years later they were in arms against the English in the cause of King Robert, when the earl was captured and hanged (thanks to his royal descent) on a gallows higher than that accorded commoner mortals.

In 1333 the earl of the day died fighting the English at Halidon Hill, and thirteen years later a successor earl (who in time became King Robert II) was in command of a Scots army at war with England. Atholl again took the field against the English at Solway Moss in the middle of the sixteenth century.

When they plotted and marched with the Jacobites, neither earl nor follower was a stranger to intrigue, or the conduct of politics by the old standby of open warfare.

During the coup that displaced James II, the game was played with a finesse appropriate to its complexity: Atholl himself went to Bath and was supposed to have no great opinion on the matter, while his eldest son declared for William and Mary but two younger sons were arrested as Jacobites.

And in 1706 (Atholl having been made a dukedom three years earlier) the duke – bitterly opposed to the projected parliamentary union with England – raised 4000 armed Atholl men at Perth, standing down his army only when it became clear that there was not enough support elsewhere in Scotland.

In the Jacobite rising of 1715, too, Atholl men played a significant part, with 1400 of them raised in four regiments under the first duke's brother (husband of the inveterate Jacobite, Lady Nairne) and three sons. One of these sons, Lord Charles, died shortly afterwards; a second, Lord George, after some time in exile, settled into three decades of safe obscurity in Perthshire. And the third, William, Marquess of Tullibardine, was deprived of his ducal inheritance by Act of (the so recently united) Parliament in London. He too would have thirty years to watch and wait (in French exile) before the chance came again.

And when it did, in 1745, neither William nor his brother George were found wanting, for once again both came out for the Jacobite cause – along with many of their immediate relations.

Indeed, old Lady Nairne – now seventy-six and as much of a Jacobite as ever – could claim with justice to have in the field not only these two nephews but two sons, four sons-in-law and six grandsons as well.

It was surely a token of the enduring loyalty that the Jacobite cause commanded, for by now James II was long dead and it was fifty-seven years since he had occupied a throne – and the early signs pointed without question to a disaster, sooner or later.

Still, it was the long-exiled William, Marquess of Tullibardine, elder brother of the Duke of Atholl, who came ashore with the Young Pretender that July, on the western shores of Lochaber. And it was Tullibardine who famously raised the Jacobite standard just one month later at nearby Glenfinnan, surrounded by the MacDonalds and Camerons who had already arrived.

Gathering support as they went, the Jacobite forces marched south, and as they approached Blair Atholl at the end of the month the 'sitting', pro-Hanoverian, duke fled to London, while Lady Nairne's daughter, Lady Lude, at once set about making the vacated castle ready for the Young Pretender. When he arrived, on the last day of August, she it was who first received him on bended knee, kissing his hand as she knelt; while the absent duke's brother, Tullibardine, claimed the ducal title of which he had been deprived after the 1715 rising.

Home at last after long exile, Tullibardine was met by 'men, women and children, who came running from their houses kissing and caressing their master whom they had not seen for thirty years', and welcomed with 'the strongest affection, which could not fail to move every generous mind with a mixture of grief and joy'.

Pausing for two days (and tasting his first-ever grouse) the twenty-four-year-old Pretender moved to a rapturous welcome in Perth, and thence to Edinburgh in the middle of September. Behind him he left a frenzy of recruiting (though in the style of the time it was not all voluntary) throughout Atholl: Lord George Murray had joined the cause; Tullibardine was rousing his brother's retainers; Stewarts and Robertsons were flocking to the standard; and all those whose names had once been MacGregor (for the name had been outlawed in 1617) were making ready to rise.

From Blair, Tullibardine sent 450 recruits to Edinburgh under the command of one of Lady Nairne's sons, and when the decision was made to invade England, an Atholl brigade of three battalions was formed. These soldiers, along with Cluny MacPherson's men, commanded by Tullibardine, were the last reinforcements to join the Jacobite army before it marched for London on the first day of November.

Just two months later, with the entourage of the Hanoverian George preparing for flight, the Jacobite army, still 5000 strong, turned back at Derby on 6 December, reached Glasgow on Boxing Day, and marched on Stirling in the middle of the following month.

Enemy forces were now closing in, and it was decided to retreat to

The Politics of the '45 Rising

The Jacobites who marched to, died on and fled from Culloden in 1746 did so in a very old cause whose roots went back at least to the early years of the previous century. For by the time of those early years King James VI of Scotland, son of Mary Queen of Scots and direct descendant of five earlier kings of his name, was poised to seize his heart's desire: the English crown.

Elizabeth I of England (no Scottish queen had ever graced the name) was ageing fast. More important, and though her enemies called her otherwise, she was the Virgin Queen – without any direct successor. And with the death in 1603 of Elizabeth (whose great virtue had nevertheless failed to dissuade her from the judicial murder of James's mother), the Scottish king did indeed take her crown, as James I of England and James VI of Scotland.

In 1625 he was succeeded by his son Charles I. But in 1649 the English executed Charles at the bidding of what by then passed as the governing authority in their country. The Scots, of whom he had been king too, at once proclaimed his heir, also the Highlands, with wheeled transport going by Blair Atholl (where the Pretender collected an additional 200 men) and the infantry by Tummel Bridge and Trinafour.

As the Jacobite forces retreated, so the government army followed. Early in February it took Perth, and within a fortnight had taken Blair Castle itself.

By now the Jacobite forces had reassembled at Inverness, and the stage was set for the most brilliant guerrilla strike of the entire campaign.

Hearing of Hanoverian depredations in Atholl and district, Tullibardine's brother, Lord George, marched with his Atholl men in extreme secrecy and at great speed for home. On the way he was joined by Cluny MacPherson and his men. Together, this 700-strong force surprised thirty armed government posts, among them important ones at Blair Inn and Bridge of Tilt.

Not one Jacobite life was lost and every Hanoverian was taken prisoner. And while Lord George had sent round Atholl the old Fiery Cross (a burning cross held aloft by a running man – the ancient

---

called Charles, as the new monarch – '*at Edinburghe crosse, the Lord Chanceler, Loudon, in black veluet goune, read the proclamatione*', quotes J. D. Mackie. Eleven years later the English found themselves in agreement with Chancellor Loudon and 'restored' Charles II to the throne.

In 1685 Charles II was succeeded by his brother, James II, a succession that triggered an orgy of political chicanery which might (or might not) shame any twentieth-century equivalent. The prevailing ideology was religious. James was a Catholic, an allegiance that gravely threatened the strategic interests of the united kingdoms. Nor did his absolutist tastes endear him to powerful interests in both Scotland and England which increasingly answered to no one but themselves.

The die was cast when, by a second wife, he fathered a son, and it became clear to his enemies that they faced a Catholic succession. Those enemies at once moved to dethrone him. He already had two children by a first marriage: Mary, married to her cousin William of Orange, and her sister Anne, married to George of Denmark. Both were Protestant in affiliation, and both loathed their father for good measure. Within months,

[Continued overleaf]

[*continued from previous page*]
therefore, William invaded England; James fled. The English
parliament claimed that he had forfeited his crown and
declared William and Mary joint sovereigns.

Two matters awaited resolution, however. The first was the
question of who was going to succeed the childless William and
Mary. And the second was that, though William was
recognized as king by both Scots and English, each nation still
had its own parliament – and there was no saying that the
Scots parliament would accept a successor proposed by the
English.

Events moved rapidly, however, and solutions were soon
devised.

William and Mary were declared king and queen in 1689,
with the agreement that should there be no heir they would be
succeeded by Anne. Five years later, Mary died without issue.
Six years after that the last of the sixteen children that Anne
had borne died too. It was promptly enacted that the

Highland way of summoning support) his men laid siege to Blair
Castle. With the garrison near to starvation, the castle might well have
fallen, but Lord George was recalled to Inverness, to which he marched
with 500 of his Atholl followers.

On 16 April the Jacobite army was decisively defeated at Culloden.
It has been calculated that every second man of the Perthshire regiments died on the field of battle or during the slaughter that followed.

According to a duke of Atholl from earlier in the present century,
there were ten officers wounded and twenty-four killed from Atholl
properties alone. Others died on the scaffold, at Penrith, York and
Kennington; while at Carlisle the Hanoverians hanged one John Mac-
Naughton on a charge of which he was patently not guilty. No bribe,
of life or money, could tempt him to betray known Jacobites, and he
died with the observation that as the Hanoverians had seen fit to class
him with gentlemen, he hoped that they would leave him to die as one
too. Others died elsewhere – not least Lord Lovat, 'Simon the Fox',
who traded barbs with the dregs of London even as he was trundled
the length of the Strand to his place of execution.

Meanwhile, the remains of the army scattered. The outlawed Mac-
Gregors marched with banners flying to their burnt homes in Balquid-

succession would now pass, after Anne, to Sophia of Hanover, a granddaughter of James I, and to her heirs. In the spring of 1702, William died and Anne took his place.

The problem of the Scots was easily dealt with. In 1707 their parliament and that of England were merged in a union which ensured a permanent English majority in the new parliament.

Gout and age respectively claimed Anne and the eighty-four-year-old Electress Sophia in 1714, when the throne passed to Sophia's heir, George I.

By now, James II was dead too. But in exile his son the Old Pretender – and in time *his* son, the Young Pretender – continued to plot: plotting that would lead to the attempts of 1715, 1719 and the final rout at Culloden. The former died in 1766, the latter in 1788 without legitimate issue, and the latter's brother in 1807.

In the words of the Scottish chancellor, Seafield, on the union of parliaments a century earlier, it was indeed the '*end of ane auld sang*'.

der and dispersed. Gaelic-speaking Lord George took what was left of his men to Badenoch and, on the orders of the Pretender, sent them off to survive as they might.

In Perthshire, as in the counties to the north, fugitives teemed in glens scavenged by troops intent on pillage and rape; while on the western coast the same fate was visited by marines hungry for blood and for the Pretender's person.

But during five months on the run he escaped betrayal or capture, and by early autumn he was back at Borrodale, in Arisaig, a mile or so from the spot at which he had landed on the Scottish mainland the previous year. From Borrodale a French ship shortly took him away to final exile.

The Hanoverian regime moved quickly to consolidate its victory. Some of the great Jacobite estates were seized; titles stripped; ancestral jurisdictions abolished; the bagpipe banned; even the wearing of the kilt forbidden.

It was the end of an old order in the Highlands. A new order, to the tunes of redcoat fife and drum, was on the way, and with it the age of emptied glens. For after Culloden the Highlands were safe for progress, transformation and the deer-forests of the nineteenth century.

 MARCH

By the beginning of March the days have lengthened a lot. By the end of the month – well, we're past the spring equinox, and whatever the weather brings, and it can still produce nasty surprises, you know that it can only get better.

And that's as well too, because March is a busy month for all of us, whether it is feeding the sheep, shooting the foxes or keeping the crows under control. And there is also heather-burning to consider as well.

By the start of the month we have got everything pretty well sussed out snow-wise. We know where the drifts are going to be, know where we are still likely to have trouble and so on, and know what sort of jobs we can attend to without trouble from the snow.

Feeding the sheep is one of the most important and perhaps the most regular of all estate jobs at this time of the year. Every morning right through to May we are feeding sheep and digging them out of any snow-drifts that they might have got into. And of course you have to keep a close eye on their general health – they are pretty heavy in lamb by now and have just come through a long, hard winter.

But if the sheep are all right, then we are up on the tops looking for foxes. It can still be very wild up there. Some of the burns can be full of snow, sometimes up to thirty feet deep, and everything is very, very solid and hard packed. In some cases you have to use crampons; we use the small instep crampons which are super little things. So off we go with the telescope and the rifle, up on the tops where you dig yourself into a bank of snow and just lie there and spy out any foxes that might be around.

This is one of the most exciting parts of the job, because if we can get the foxes now – well, it will save the lives of an awful lot of young grouse and lambs later on in the year.

Of course, it has been a long, hard winter for the fox too – and the vixens are carrying their young by now as well. So they are always on the prowl looking for this or that, looking for anything at all that might be worth eating. It is us against them – and it's a pretty equal contest. We have these white suits, our snow-suits, and we get into a position which gives a proper angle of fire and make sure the wind is in the right direction, because the fox is really switched on.

I suppose these suits give us something of an advantage really, because the fox doesn't change his colour in winter like some other animals.

If you are lucky you can get three in a day, but most times you are pleased to get one, and some days you will go out and get nothing at all – it is all a matter of luck. You often have a good idea if they are around, mind you. You know from previous years where they tend to be, and you can see the marks of them, so you just get into position and spy for them with the 'scope. Basically, you are just a fox sniper – stalking and sniping the foxes on the high ground above Glen Tilt.

Getting them on the low ground is a different matter, of course, because you can't stalk and snipe in wooded ground. So you drive them out of the woods, just by walking through the trees and talking loudly, or perhaps firing the odd shot in the air to frighten them. And we can also use dogs – they will soon frighten any foxes out of the woods, and as soon as they are driven out we shoot them.

Culling foxes is a continuous job for a gamekeeper, and it doesn't matter how many times you think they are beautiful, cuddly animals – there are a lot of them out there, and their numbers must be controlled. The country fox is the same species as the town fox, but otherwise it is a different animal.

And low-ground foxes are a bit different to high-ground foxes too. The low-ground ones are semi-streetwise, but the high-ground foxes are really very wild. They hate to see anyone; they hate humans, hate us. They will smell you from half a mile away and that's it – they are gone in a flash. They lie and watch you and will then slink off into the rocks and disappear.

View near Blair Atholl

They can do an awful lot of damage if they get off with it. I know some farmers who have lost maybe sixty lambs in one season, and that's a lot of money down the drain. Mind you, it doesn't matter how many foxes we take out; there are always more of them. It's not as if we were exterminating them – it's hard enough just trying to control their numbers.

Don't get me wrong. I have great respect for foxes. I think every keeper respects them. But I suppose we hate them at the same time. When you go into a pheasant pen and you see fifty young pheasants killed and left where they died, then you don't have too many warm feelings for a fox. The fact is that the fox is a very, very wild animal.

The fox loves to kill lambs, and that's where we come in. He usually grabs them at the back of the neck, one or two crunches and they are dead. Then the fox will go and cut the tail off, cut it off quite cleanly, and then the head comes off, the nose, the ears – they can make a terrible mess, almost as if it were for the fun of it. They will maybe kill four lambs and take nothing but the head of one of them. And next day they will kill another four. Day after day, they will be killing until you get them with the rifle.

And it can mean an awful lot of time on the hill for us, because the best time to get them is very early in the morning, which means we have to be out on the hill all night.

It's the same with the birds – they can cause a lot of damage, although these days a lot of them are protected, and any keeper stupid enough to even think of killing them would be dismissed from his job at once. If you are caught destroying them then it is guaranteed that your job is on the line. You are told that when you are first employed. You must do as best you can with the lawful resources at your disposal, which means that only some species of bird can be shot or trapped.

The crows are the worst of the lot. They have terrific eyesight and are not easy to catch at all. The best way is to get them at the nest. They will eat just about anything – dead hares, dead rabbits, dead deer. Even a fish left at the river bank will be taken by the crows if they have a chance.

So we shoot them whenever and wherever we can. They are terrible for robbing the nests of other birds. They will just stab their beak into an egg and fly home with it for their own young. They sit up at the edge of the nest and empty the egg out. You sometimes see fifty or more shells around a crow's nest. Crows are dreadful news for curlews in particular. Nowadays, there are areas where there used to be a lot of curlews and there are none now, because the crows have driven them out. So we try to destroy their nests along with their young, or else we can try to trap the adults.

I mean, there's no way we will ever wipe them out. There are less and less keepers around, and everyone tries to control crow numbers within the law, so there's no chance of them ever being wiped out.

Sometimes we use traps and they are very good; they work very well, but we can work them only at certain times of the year and in certain areas.

They are roughly a three-foot-square net and wire cage – two entrances from either the side or the top, with a trigger. And, of course, a bird is needed inside it to attract the crow, which is a territorial creature. When he comes back to his nest and finds a strange bird below it he will fly down to investigate, to fight this stranger and drive him away or kill him. And that way he gets caught, of course, because once he goes into the trap he can't get back out again.

And as well as trying to keep down the foxes and the crows, and feeding the sheep, there is always heather-burning to be attended to, of course, although that depends on how much snow is left on the ground; sometimes it could be later in the year. Ideally, it is done on a seven-year cycle. If you get a good, hot fire on old heather you can burn it to the ground, completely obliterate it, and that allows the growth of young heather, which is important for the grouse because that is what they live on.

We don't burn it all at once, naturally. You burn it in strips to get a sequence of different types and ages of heather, a bit like a patchwork quilt. You need some old heather to give shelter for the grouse as well. You also want patches of hill which are wettish to give them a bit of drinking water, somewhere they can find dew in the early morning.

And there have to be places where there are plenty of bugs to be found, because that is what young grouse live on for the first ten to fifteen days of their lives. Obviously, young grouse can't fly, so they have to survive on what they can catch on the ground.

Mind you, if there has been a long winter and a lot of late frost that doesn't help with the bugs – and that can result in great loss. The hen can be sitting and hatching out all the young and they suddenly die one by one because there is not enough feeding for them. It happens, and it happens quite often.

Obviously, burning the heather also allows grass and flowers to grow, which is good news for the sheep, and for the deer too, come to think of it. And sphagnum moss is on the go at this time of the year too. It's a hill plant, and as far back as anyone can remember it has been used for many things. One of its main uses was on wounds, because it is iodine-based.

During the First World War things were so bad that that was all they had. Women were out on the hills gathering big baskets of sphagnum moss for the wounded troops – that was the only dressing they had available at the time. Mind you, it has other uses too. If the men are on the hill there is obviously no toilet available, so we always look for a small patch of sphagnum moss because it is very hygienic – and doesn't cost the same as that stuff you see on the television advertisements with the dog!

So heather-burning is a very important form of land management, though you have to be very careful about when you do it. Naturally, you can't burn the heather when there is any risk of ground-nesting birds sitting on their nests. The higher the area is, the less chance you have of getting the ground-nesters.

You need a team of strong, young lads for the job, armed with besoms – those are big brushes for beating out the fires. And you need to take great care that a fire never gets out of control. You calculate the direction in which the wind will blow it, and choose a patch which has a natural firebreak in the background, maybe a burn or a rock-face or something like that.

You start the fire with a small paraffin-operated heather-burner across a distance of anything from fifteen to fifty yards, with beaters posted on either side to make sure that the fire burns in the

The River Tilt in full spate

intended direction. You just keep it in a straight line until it comes to the stream or rock-face and then you try to put it out. That can be hard work, and you can get a lot of blisters on your hands. Some people wear gloves, but that is for pansies!

So all things considered, by the end of March we have had a busy few weeks – burning the moor to let the young heather come on, keeping the sheep in good condition, and trying to keep down the numbers of foxes and crows. Because by then we're getting closer to the time when there is going to be an awful lot of young crows, foxes and lambs about: and all of them very hungry. But everyone knows that the coming weeks, with the longer days and better weather on offer, will be even busier than they have been. From now on there isn't much let-up at all for any of us.

Wildlife, Wild Glen

G len Tilt and the district of Blair Atholl in general has historically teemed with a wide range of animals and birds.
According to the author of *The Old Statistical Account* (1791):

> *In an extensive forest, and over many other parts of the hill, there are a great number of red deer; in and near the woods, there are roe-deer; almost everywhere there are plenty of hares, and, on the high mountains, white hares, which, in summer, have bluish spots. In the hills and woods are foxes wild cats, polecats, martens, weasels and shrew mice; in the waters, otters. We have also two species of badger. Of the winged kind there are, on the tops of the mountains, ptarmigans; in the hills, grouse; near the woods, black game, and partridges below. The ravenous birds are eagles, buzzards, hawks of various kinds, ravens, carrion crows, and magpies. The migratory birds are similar to those usual in the Highlands.*

And by the time of *The New Statistical Account* (1845) the wildlife of the district was scarcely any less rich:

> *It is said that there are 7000 red deer in the Atholl Forest, and the number is not over-rated, if the extent of ground, of which they have the undisturbed possession, be any criterion. The roe-deer also are numerous in the different plantations of the country. The fox, the wild cat, the marten, the polecat, the weasel and the Alpine hare are common. The rabbit, the squirrel and the rat have lately made their way into the country. The eagle has his eyrie in the mountains of the Atholl Forest. The kestrel builds his nest in Glen Tilt, and at the Falls of the Bruar. Red and black game, the ptarmigan and the plover, and partridges, are plentiful. The oyster-catcher comes up the Garry towards the end of March and nestles upon its gravelly bank.*

Of course, this was before – just before – the huge destruction of wildlife that accompanied the development of Highland sporting estates in the middle of the nineteenth century.

> *My colleague on that occasion shot the dog fox at
> 3.25 a.m. and I bagged the vixen, whom I had
> heard start skirling soon after the shot which had
> killed her mate, ten minutes later as she ran past me,
> still wailing. If ever I heard a note of absolute anguish
> it was in the keening of that vixen. I would swear to
> this day that she had seen her mate killed, knew that
> her cubs were lost to her, and was leaving the scene of
> the disaster keening in irrepressible misery.*
>
> Lea MacNally, *Highland Year*

James Barron's *The Northern Highlands in the Nineteenth Century*
records that on just one estate – Glengarry – between 1837 and 1840 the
following were destroyed:

11 foxes	5 marsh harriers	3 honey buzzards
198 wild cats	63 goshawks	462 kestrels
246 martens	285 common	78 merlins
106 polecats	buzzards	83 hen harriers
27 sea-eagles	371 rough-leg	6 gyr falcons
15 golden eagles	buzzards	1431 hooded crows
18 ospreys	301 stoats and	475 ravens
98 blue hawks	weasels	35 horned owls
7 orange-leg	67 badgers	71 fern owls
falcons	48 otters	3 golden owls
11 hobby hawks	78 housecats (gone	8 magpies
275 kites	wild)	

Thus was room made in the Highlands for wildlife judged 'sporting',
such as grouse and deer.

But in Atholl today, wildlife is plentiful and includes not only red
deer but also roe- and fallow-deer, otters, foxes, pine martens, wild cats
and blue and brown hares. Among the birds are grouse, ptarmigan,
capercaillie, blackcock, various types of hawks including the kestrel,
buzzards and eagles. The oyster-catcher still comes up the Garry
(despite the predations of black-headed gulls); the osprey in season
also now visits (or visits again) and is pleased to poach a favoured pool
or two on the Tilt.

Many of these birds have charmed naturalists in the past, as, indeed,
they continue to do today.

For instance, the Victorian naturalist and deer-stalker Charles St
John writes in *The Wild Sports of the Highlands* (1924) of a 'pet'
peregrine he had.

Wildlife: Wild Glen

For the first year the bird was of a dark brown colour above, with longitudinal spots on the feathers of her breast. On changing her plumage during the second autumn of her existence, she became of a most beautiful dark slate colour above, and the spots of her breast turned into cross bars, every feather being barred with black; her throat became of a beautiful cream colour. With great strength, she is possessed of the most determined courage, and will attack any person or dog who she takes a dislike to. Her poultry-killing propensities oblige me to keep her chained in the

Red grouse A gamebird. Dark red-brown plumage with darker mottlings, and blackish tail and wingtips; whitish feathered legs; cock has prominent red wattle over eye. Typical calls are a loud 'kok-kok-kok' and 'goback-goback'; and various other notes associated with courtship. Its habitat is moors, bogs or mosses with heather or crowberry (not grass).

Ptarmigan A member of the grouse family, its plumage in winter is all white, except for black lores (cock only) and tail. Black bill, feathered legs; red wattle over eye. Its voice is a hoarse croak. Its habitat is barren, rocky mountain-tops, usually above 2500 feet and rarely below 2000 feet. Confined to the highest Scottish mountains.

Capercaillie Also a member of the grouse family. Cock is blackish-grey, with green throat and upper breast, brown wing-coverts and white on flanks. Cock has a raucous cry, and an almost indescribable song that starts with a resonant rattle and ends with a sound like drawing a cork and pouring liquid out of a narrow-necked bottle, followed by a crashing sound made by scraping wing feathers on the ground.

Blackcock The male of the black grouse. Cock is black-glossed dark blue (black-brown during brief autumnal eclipse), with white wing-bar and under tail-coverts, and lyrate tail. In movement, flight intermediate between capercaillie and red grouse. More gregarious than capercaillie; in spring and to lesser extent in autumn large gatherings occur at communal display ground called 'lek'.

Abstracted from *Collins Pocket Guide to British Birds*

kitchen-garden, where no other bird, except a tame owl, resides.
The owls she appears to tolerate with great good nature.

And Darling writes in a lyrical vein about both red and black grouse.
Of the former, he notes:

> *The life history of the red grouse is that of a bird excelling in*
> *hardiness. Surely the ptarmigan is the only other bird which can*
> *exist in more unsheltered and inclement conditions. When the*
> *snow falls heavily and without wind, the grouse will move*
> *elsewhere, but if there is sufficient wind to keep patches of heather*
> *and grit clear of snow, the grouse will stay where they are. The*
> *birds move upwards immediately the snow begins to melt.*

And he adds, '*The hen grouse at all times sits close [on her eggs] and*
may herself be buried for a day or two under snow, but in winter grouse as
a species do not get snowed up as sheep do under a peat hag. The birds
tread with their feet all the time and rise with the snow.'

The same writer describes a form of moorland discothèque favoured
by the black grouse. He says, '*The black grouse is a species in which the*
males gather at traditional places in spring and join in ceremonial posturing.
This dancing ground is called the "lek". It is after these meetings and
stimulating evolutions of the male birds in concert that mating takes place
with the hens, which are not far away.'

But of all these birds of hill or moor, whether predator or game, the
eagle must be considered monarch, on account of its size no less than its
majesty in flight, and its fierce, predatory manners.

A member of the hawk family, and sometimes pale-headed, with a rich
brown plumage, it has a dark hooked bill, yellow feet and feathered legs.
In flight it is the most majestic of birds, given to soaring and gliding, its
wing tips splayed and upturned, with a lazy style of effortless grace.

> *Contrary in habit to the fox, the stag always*
> *runs up the wind, that he may discover and*
> *shun his enemy: the crafty fox, as if sensible to the*
> *infamy of his trail, never moves by day, unless*
> *pursued, and flies down the wind, that, by taking his*
> *scent with him, he may leave as little as possible to*
> *betray his course.*
>
> J. S. Stuart and C. E. Stuart, *Lays of the Deer Forest*

Wildlife: Wild Glen

> ❀ *Deer, like sheep, tend to move around the
> countryside on historically proven routes;
> hill-walkers often find the deer-trots constitute the
> best way across a gully or awkward defile.*
>
> Michael Wigan, *Stag at Bay*

Of all the raptorial birds, it has seduced observers more than any others – and little wonder in that.

A pair hunt as a rule over some 11 000 acres in the eastern Highlands (the figure rises to around 18 000 in the west), according to Darling, and their principal foods include '*mountain hare, red grouse, ptarmigan, rabbit and carrion, mostly of red deer and sheep. Fox, stoat, weasel, crow, pigeon, caper, blackcock, pheasant, wild ducks, gulls, fulmar, shearwater, waders, red deer and roe-deer calves and lambs (mostly as carrion) also form a proportion of the eagle's diet*'.

It is therefore something of an ambiguous friend to the sporting estate, as an enemy of game, vermin and livestock alike, but few professional hill-men have been able to resist its charms.

MacNally recalls in *Highland Year* an incident when he was hind-stalking one day:

> *Walking along the path midway up one side of a tree-clad, river-bottomed glen I saw deer begin to pour over the skyline of the opposite side of the glen and run in a panic-stricken ragged bunch into the trees below. There they scattered and stood beneath the bare branches while I wondered exceedingly. And then there floated lazily, and, it seemed, almost insolently, into view above that skyline first one, then another, eagle. This then was what had stampeded the deer down into the shelter of the trees, knowing full well that they were safe there from the eagle's swoop. That the eagle will kill deer calves I know, but I doubt if it will often attempt seriously to attack an adult deer. Nevertheless, the ingrained fear is there.*

And if the eagle is king of the birds on a modern sporting estate, then the red deer is king of the beasts that are to be found there. These are not the monster deer of prehistoric times, but the red deer of today are still pretty impressive beasts, roaming over huge tracts of the Scottish Highlands, on land – or much of it – which is not suited (unless heavily subsidized) to the farming of sheep, or anything else for that matter.

Wildlife: Wild Glen

> *Listen, don't pay any attention to them
> naturalists who say the stag, or the eagle, or
> whatever is king of the glen. That's rubbish – there's
> only one king of the glen, and that's the midgie.
> A pure bastard – though I wouldn't call it that in
> public, of course.*
>
> Anon

They are, by nature, territorial creatures, and every herd of hinds will have its own range, covering anything from one square mile to four or five square miles. No matter how large or small an area it is, the deer will know it with an intimacy that few stalkers could manage – its gullies and burns, its woods and wallows, its open moorland and high corries.

They will know the weather of their home range intimately too, sometimes demonstrating an uncanny ability to predict the advent of heavy weather, moving down from the high tops ahead of a storm, or moving back up again if they know a spell of good winter weather is on the way. As a rule they will spend their time on low ground in winter and move high into the hills during the summer, to keep clear of flies and other naturally occurring pests (among which they might well have reason to number man).

As a species they have a distinct style of social organization, the sexes living apart for ten or eleven months out of each year. The stags, in loose groupings, occupy the tops of the mountains; the hinds, their calves, and most one- or two-year-old stags in their own much more closely knit communities stay on lower ground.

The hinds are notably graceful creatures and highly inquisitive.

According to the Stuarts in *Lays of the Deer Forest*, if a hunter remains absolutely motionless, an intrigued hind will come very close.

> *Sometimes, when suspicious, and uncertain of his appearance,
> they exhibit an amusing indecision between curiosity and appre-
> hension, and if the waiter is dressed in dusky tartan, or an
> aerial, brown, or wan-green colour, will advance within a few
> yards of his post. We have seen a hind approach within twenty
> paces of a figure standing against a rock. She was however certain
> that there was something – perhaps she remembered that the craig
> did not used to have that dun scaur on its face – but she could
> not make out what it was, and was very curious to know; trotting*

Wildlife: Wild Glen

up within a few yards of the waiter, stretching her neck and ears, and feeling the air with her nose, as if she tried to squeeze a scent out of it: then retreating, and moving quickly to the left and right, in order to get the wind of the object which she suspected, and when all failed, advancing as before, close up to the gun. Upon these occasions the hunter must maintain a petrified stability; for even the motion of his features is sometimes sufficient to give conviction to the deer.

They are also extremely suspicious creatures, depending greatly on a highly developed sense of smell and hearing. Some natural noises they might overlook, but the clink of a rifle or nailed boot on rock, or the sudden alarm of a bird or sheep, and they will at once be on the alert, with that sudden head-up pose that has been the despair of out-of-range stalkers over generations.

Each year the breeding ritual is the same. In late summer the stags are still high in the mountains. In April their antlers will have fallen off; by August their antlers have regrown, and the stags are ready for the contest of the rut. And towards the end of September, one by one, they leave the corries in search of the herds of hinds and followers.

This is the time of the roaring, when the stags exhibit elaborate display behaviour with each other, and there's occasional serious fighting, while they try to capture and hold a group of hinds – fighting off as they do the attentions of other stags. By the end of October the rut is finished, and stags and hinds separate for the rest of the year.

All winter they remain apart, and in late May and early June the dappled calves are born and hidden in the heather until able to follow their mothers. But their youth is short and cruel: by August the dapples have gone, they are about to witness their first rut. And then there is the winter, in which four out of every ten will die – more, if the winter is a fierce one.

For the stags, the hinds and their followers, in short, winter is the hardest of times – and on an estate that does not control their numbers by culling, harder than ever.

❧ APRIL ❧

Let me tell you now about something that is maybe the most important of all things to a gamekeeper's work. It's maybe not the sort of thing that comes to mind as that – but it is, all the same. Without it we just wouldn't be able to begin to do the work – and that's the clothes we wear, and the gear we need to go to the hill in the sort of weather we get in Glen Tilt.

And I suppose we should start with the one item of clothing that people would associate with gamekeeping above all – the tweed plus-four suit of jacket, waistcoat, hat and trousers. I don't suppose you actually see many of them around the cities, but they are just the thing for the hills around here.

If you are a keeper, the plus-four suit goes with the job. It is part of your wages, and these days a good plus-four suit probably costs up to £500. But they are worth it.

For instance, the jacket has all the pockets you would ever need. Usually, there are poachers' pockets on the left-hand side which can hold at least two pheasants, folded up with the head under the wing. There is always room for your 'piece' as well – I suppose the proper name for it is packed lunch, but piece is what we call it here. You also have room to carry extra cartridges, a smallish waterproof coat – even a half-bottle of whisky if you feel like having something to warm you up.

When they are wet, the jackets do sometimes feel a bit uncomfortable, but at least they keep you warm, and that is very important in the wintertime. On the hill there is very little shelter, so you must be able to depend on your clothes to keep you warm. It is bad enough getting cold, but then there is wind-chill to consider, and that really can do you damage, so it is extremely important to have a good jacket.

People who aren't used to them sometimes wonder why they have the gussets which run down the back between the shoulder-blades to the top of the hip. Well, of course, that is to allow you to raise your arms when you are actually shooting with overhead, outstretched arms – you should find them on any well-made plus-four suit.

Traditionally, too, the waistcoat was part of the suit, though they are not worn so much today. I think they were maybe more of a badge of office for the head keeper, so he could have a watch-chain and a watch across the breast of it. It is quite a handy thing, with useful wee pockets – though these days tweed waistcoats are a bit out of fashion.

They are being replaced by sleeveless bodywarmers, usually made in thermal synthetic fibre, quilted duck-down or waxed cotton. Whichever kind it is, your arms are free to swing, lift game-bags, shoot. They are very handy in summer, and I have one or two of them myself.

The trousers are an essential part of the suit too, naturally. Like the jacket, they too have a multitude of deep pockets, where you can carry your knife and all the other bits of gear that you might need on the hill. They usually have two big hip pockets – and I have even heard of some keepers down south who have a special truncheon-pocket down the right-hand seam of the trousers. Some of these guys need these things. Up here, luckily, we don't need them – well, not so much, anyway.

Mind you, they're not in fact trousers but breeches, fastened below the knee with a buckle or something like that, and with a fold of cloth hanging down below that for four inches. They are just the thing for the hill; they are super for walking through heather. And the fold of cloth at the knee means that when you are crawling or even walking they sort of ride up and down on your knee and leave plenty of space for movement. They're not like normal trousers which, when they get wet, grip round your legs and wear down the skin – something that is not very comfortable after a while!

The tweed itself is obviously unique to the estate; it is really a sort of identity badge. Other estates have a different sort of tweed for their suits, and sometimes you will see keepers from other parts

Charlie and a friend on a grouse shoot. Charlie is
wearing a sleeveless bodywarmer and plus-fours

of the country and you can tell at once where they come from because of the tweed they are wearing.

One estate round here, for example, uses a sort of bright blue colour. You would think it would stand out, and indeed it does at close range. But at a distance of half a mile it looks grey. It blends incredibly well against a rocky face; unless the person moves you would need a pair of binoculars to spot them.

Here on Atholl, we use a tweed which is composed of small, square checks. If we are lying in the grass, we are very hard to see because of the grey-green mixture in the tweed. It is very good camouflage, and that of course is a big help to a stalker or a keeper on the hill, or in woods, out looking for poachers, or whatever job he is doing.

Animals and birds also get used to us wearing the same colour of clothes, of course. If a keeper has been feeding young pheasants for a while, brought them on from the time they were a day old, then they will actually think he is an entirely other person if he turns up in different clothes. You really have to wear the same clothes all the time – the same colour of clothes – so that they get used to it. It makes the job a lot easier at times, believe me.

With deer, naturally, it is a different story. Deer just don't want to see you ever, so, with them, you have to depend on the tweed to act as a top-class sort of camouflage garment.

Plus-fours absolutely keep you warm in winter; but the funny thing is they also keep you cool in the summertime – I don't know why, but that is certainly the case. They are really wonderful things for the hill. Mind you, you have to be careful that you don't tighten the breeches too much on top of your calf below the knee: a few years of that, and you could end up with a bad case of varicose veins. That's why buckles are good. The likes of modern stick-on contact fasteners, on the other hand, are absolutely hopeless, especially when you are crawling. They just slip off, and the deep fold of cloth is half-way down to your ankles. And the only time you ever need them like that is when you are soaking wet if you have crossed a burn and you are up to your waist in water. And by God, we are often like that on the hill. There are many, many stalkers who will confirm that to you!

So when you are going to be in deep water, you unbuckle the

breeches and they hang down very loosely round the legs. That takes the weight of the water off the upper part of the breeches round your thighs and hips, and lets it drain away quickly. After all, it is not a good thing to let your legs stay wet for any length of time, year in, year out: you will end up with arthritis and rheumatics. So you unbuckle the breeches to let them drain, and leave them unbuckled to let the air at your legs – and naturally any wind will dry your legs and the breeches quite quickly.

So plus-fours have a long future ahead of them. And these days there are patent waterproof linings for them, which make a big difference. I amn't saying it will be absolutely foolproof, but it will certainly be a terrific help in keeping your legs and knees dry – and that is a very important thing indeed.

Now, I have spoken about the importance of the right footwear – mountain-shoes, -boots – earlier, but naturally you're just wasting your time if you don't have the right socks for the right footwear: or stockings, if we are talking about wearing plus-fours.

Indeed, stockings are even more important when it comes to the kilt. With good stockings, you can pull the tops up over your knees when you are crawling and that will give some protection. Not that I would ever favour the kilt for stalking. I have tried it, right enough, but it's no fun crawling through rocks. Most of us here still have kilts and we can be wearing them at the grouse sometimes. But for stalking, though I have worn the kilt, give me plus-fours and good stockings any time.

Naturally, you will not want to hold them up with elastic or stuff like that. If it is too tight, over the years you'll get varicose veins. So I turn down the stockings three or four inches over a knitted sort of garter, about an inch wide by eighteen inches long, which I wind lightly round my legs. That's the best thing for keeping the stockings up, whether worn with plus-fours or kilt.

In the old days, of course, you didn't wear anything under the kilt. But in our own times there's always plenty to be put on under the plus-fours, especially in cold weather.

For instance, tights are very warm and are recommended if you have to be lying out all night in the winter in a tent or sleeping-bag. Twenty-odd years ago there were none of these new thermals around, but the string vest really did work. It seemed to trap warm air under the shirt, and made a huge difference. As for the shirt – in summery weather a light short-sleeved one will do the job. But in winter you want something that you can get right up around your throat, up to the edge of your ears and right down your back to protect the internal organs. I always tell the boys in the bothy that these are the things they should be wanting for Christmas presents and not hankies and the likes of that. Good clothing is of the very first importance on the hill, because your life could some day depend on it.

Now, there are other bits and pieces which are essential kit for the hill: the deerstalker, the crook – that's what we call a long walking-stick – and, sometimes, gloves and balaclavas.

You can get the deerstalker in two styles: with a stiff, stitched brim, or the traditional Sherlock Holmes kind, with the ear-flaps and a peak at the front and the back. I usually prefer the former, because as often as not you can crumple it up and stick it in a pocket. And, unlike an ordinary cap, the brim runs the water over the back of your neck, rather than down it. It's wee things like that which make all the difference on the hill, believe me.

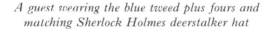

A guest wearing the blue tweed plus fours and matching Sherlock Holmes deerstalker hat

But there are times when the flapped bonnet comes into its own. They are warm, for one thing. By the time of the last few weeks of the stag-stalking, we usually find that we are grateful for them, because it is that damn cold on the hill and you can tie it over your ears for warmth. And the chin-strap stops it getting blown away too – well, it does if you have actually tied it! It is also very useful at the heather-burning: you can turn it side-on and keep the heat of the flames away from your face. It is also handy for carrying eggs in. If you come over a pheasant's nest, you can pick up the eggs in the hat and you have two ready-made handles; it's a bit like a basket.

You can use it for other things too. Say you come across a trapped fox: you can use the traditional deerstalker to protect your hand when you grab it by the nose and avoid getting bitten. Or say you are camped out on the hill: the deerstalker is just the thing for lifting your billy-can off the fire. When you are stalking, it keeps the sun out of your eyes. Say you are crawling up to a ridge and the sun is dead ahead and low in the sky: when you spy over the edge, the sun doesn't get into your eyes. Being tweed and in the colours of the countryside, it is also very good camouflage. It also helps hide the face, and this is very important too, because almost all animals can detect movement. If they see any part of your face or your hair, they always seem to twig right away. And, of course, the deerstalker is waterproof nearly always – so it is a very, very versatile piece of equipment.

To tell you the truth, when I get a new set of plus-fours, I always go for an extra deerstalker rather than a waistcoat. I go through a lot of hats. They either get burnt drying off at a fire, or they get lost or something, or the wind blasts them away to goodness knows where. So I always go for the deerstalker rather than the waistcoat.

Now, another thing essential on the hill is the crook. I personally have two or three of them. I use them almost every day we go on the hill. It is part of your dress, plus the fact that it can be used for so many things – it is almost as versatile as the deerstalker.

Obviously, it is a walking aid. It helps keep you on your feet on rocks and in deep heather, for a start. You can use it for wading rivers; first gauge the depth with it, and then you can wade while the stick holds you against the current. You can pull people up bankings. If you have a guest who is maybe a wee bit frail or older, you haul them up – or indeed help lower them down a slope. If they need a crook and don't have one, one can always lend it to them too.

In boggy conditions, moss or peat bogs, it will give you an idea of how solid the ground is – is it safe to walk on, is it too deep? It will even give you an idea if the ground is safe for horses, though of course they weigh a lot more so you have to be careful there. You can also put a snare on the end of a crook, and pull a salmon out of a pool. Or you can put a bit of barbed wire on the end and maybe drive a fox out of a hole.

And you can leave it on the hill pointing in the direction you have taken, so that a pony-man can know where to find you. And it is absolutely essential when it comes to working with sheep – that's why it has the big hooked handle, to snap round the neck of a sheep and capture it.

You can also use it for hanging your billy-can over a fire, or just holding it over a fire until it boils. And you can use it as a rest for the telescope when you are glassing the hill for deer or foxes, or put it under your arm and it steadies you if you are using binoculars.

Making crooks is a pretty specialized job. You need the right size and age of hazel-wood for the stick itself. It must be just the correct length, not too long or short, not too thick or thin, so it is just right for your height and the grip of your hand. It is cut, and dried for maybe two or three years before it is finished.

Then the maker puts on the handle. That's made from the horn of a tup; the horn of the black-faced tup is about the best. Once it is cut down to size, it is boiled and so on. There are various tricks the makers have, but you don't hear too much about them; they all have their own little secrets. George, our shepherd down the glen, he makes very good working sticks, while some guys specialize in very decorative ones – not really the sort of thing you would take to the hill.

Some guys like to put a thistle on the top, for instance. Others put a turn-up on the end of the handle – no, not a neep, but a turn-up – so that the handle doesn't snag in the wool when you catch a sheep. You can find lots of other designs too – the heads of sheep, dogs, pheasants, otters, badgers and so on. And then you polish

Carn a' Chlamain, above Glen Tilt

them all up. You can get some really beautiful ones. You can see them at game fairs and country shows – some of them costing up into the hundreds.

But like most stalkers, I just have working sticks, and if one gets broken you don't grieve too much – though you do get quite fond of an individual crook. After all, it spends an awful lot of time on the hill with you and you do depend on it a lot.

Given some of the frost and snow conditions we can get in Glen Tilt, there's also many a day on the hill when you need gloves. I like best a nice thermal inner glove under long-arm mitts with a good gripping palm and a bungee to close them and keep the snow out. They are quick to come off too, and that is important. Sometimes I just use one, unless the conditions are really atrocious. Crawling in on hinds, say, I always like to have my shooting hand free, and when you are using a walking-stick you usually want a bare hand on it, for a good, safe grip. You must have the gloves attached to your jacket, mind you, like when you were a kid, and your mum used to thread a piece of string up one sleeve, round your neck, and down the other sleeve, each end tied to a glove, so you couldn't lose them.

A full-face balaclava is sometimes worth while too, because it has two uses. If it just shows the eyes and nose it is very good camouflage, just the thing for a long wait at the nest of a hoodie crow or a fox's den, because the white of your face is easily enough to give you away. And in snowstorm conditions, in a blizzard, when the snow is in your nose, ears, eyes, it can help keep it out. And it can also help keep the wind from going down your throat, and deep inside your clothes.

Of course, in these sorts of conditions you aren't in the plus-fours any more, or at least you are also wearing additional protective clothing for the conditions.

For blizzard conditions, you really must make sure that you are kitted out properly. You'll maybe want the likes of a thermal vest, wristwarmers, a nice thick woollen sweater and some sort of bodywarmer waistcoat. You will also obviously need to have an outer waterproof suit of some kind, a jacket or coat and trousers or leggings, both almost certainly dark green in colour.

There are so many types available that it is entirely a matter of choice, but it is important that the zips are all flapped over and that all seams are taped and sealed. Myself, I like a jacket or coat long enough to cover the small of your back, keep your kidneys warm, and indeed right down to the hips. This is very important, I think, because stalkers are crawling about a lot in bad mountain weather, and it does affect them eventually.

And, of course, they will need a hood or a high collar. I wouldn't wear a hood unless it was absolutely necessary, but I do have hoods on two of my jackets and I have been glad of them at times. But they do restrict your hearing, if you are listening, say, to the stags roaring at the rut. If there is a wind blowing, it gets inside the hood and blanks out any other noise. And a hood can also restrict your side vision quite badly. That's why most times I prefer a very high collar and, provided you don't get agitated with it rubbing against your ears or the back of your head, it can be very wind-proofing and keep the cold out.

Of course, when conditions are really bad up the glen, then you sometimes need every bit of kit you can get your hands on. Another thing I wear, and it is sort of mandatory for the bothy lads, is what we call instep crampons. These aren't the full-blown big climbing jobs, but little ones which buckle around the instep of your boot. They fit nicely in front of the heel and tighten up with nylon straps. When you are on a snowy or icy face on the hill, they give fantastic support and grip. They are something I issue to all the boys that go stalking here when conditions get like that.

And if it is really very bad, and I still have to get on with outside work, then I have seen myself having to use snow-goggles.

Kitted up like that, I suppose I must look a bit like a spaceman or something. But believe me, by the end of that sort of day's weather, I am more like a snowman. And more to the point, I have been reasonably warm and dry all day, and am still alive and well – which is not something that you can ever absolutely guarantee on the Scottish hills in winter.

The Fare of Keepers
and Kings

In the history of Highland deer-forests, the destruction of game and its consumption with orgiastic relish march hand in zealous hand, whether outdoors or in, whether at morning, noon or night

Lindsay of Pitscottie's account of hunting in Glen Tilt includes a description of the lavish hospitality provided in 1528 by the Earl of Atholl for his guests, King James V, the king's mother and an ambassador of the Pope.

> *The earl made such provision for the king and his mother and the ambassador, that they had all manner of meats, drinks and delicacies that were to be gotten at that time in all Scotland, either in town or country. That is to say, all kind of drink, such as ale, beer, wine, both white and claret, madeira, sweet muscatel, spiced hippocras, and strong spirits. Further, there were all types of breads and meats: beef, mutton, lamb, veal, venison, sucking pigs, chicken and rabbits; along with goose, heron, swan, partridge, plover, duck, drake, turkey, peacock, black-cock, grouse, and capercaillie. The surrounding ponds were full of delicious fishes, such as salmon, trout, perch, pike, eel, and the other sorts of fish to be had in fresh water: and all ready for the banquet. There were also special stewards, skilled bakers, cooks and chefs, with cakes and sweets for their desserts.*

And in 1618 the Earl of Mar took a distinguished (and vast) party on a shooting expedition, in the company of John Taylor. Taylor later recalled:

> *The kitchen was always on the side of a bank, many kettles and pots boiling, and many spits turning and winding, with great variety of cheer, such as venison, baked, boiled, or roast; and stewed beef, mutton, goats, kids, hares, fresh salmon, pigeons, hens, capons, chickens, partridges, cootes, heath-cocks, capercaillies, and ptarmigans; good ale, sherry, white wine, claret, sweet red tent, and most potent spirits. Thus a company of about 1400 was most amply fed.*

The Fare of Keepers and Kings

By the time that Victoria and her 'dear, dear' Prince Albert had established themselves at Balmoral, however, shooting-party dishes were French in style, and as a natural consequence were much more civilized (though oddly non-alcoholic). For luncheon, according to Duff Hart-Davis, Albert and his guests would typically enjoy the following sort of menu, sent out to them at their sport:

> *Homard naturel, sauce rémoulade*
> *Ragoût de mouton provençal*
> *Poulet et langue à l'Anglaise*
> *Salade Vosigienne*
> *Epinards au beurre*
> *Pommes de terre maître d'hôtel*
> *Tarte aux framboises et groseilles*
> *Compote de pêches.*

English cuisine was not, of course, overlooked, and on this particular menu was nobly represented by what is described as pouding au riz and, finally, apple dumpling – clearly a concept that the gracious subtleties of the French language were unable to encompass.

Naturally, this luncheon was for the dozen or so 'rifles' only. The retainers – beaters, stalkers, pony-men and the rest – ate more modestly.

Breakfast, too, in a Victorian shooting-lodge was a sturdy affair. J. G. Bertam, writing in 1889 in his *Outdoor Sports in Scotland*, recalls with lusty precision one such meal; one can only regret the absence of a companion volume on Scottish indoor sports, overeating evidently among them.

> *Happily, I started with the best of all foundations, a capital*
> *breakfast. Attend and envy me: item first, a steak of broiled*
> *salmon; item second, a helping from a pie composed of jellied*
> *sheep's head nicely seasoned and palatable; item third, a savoury*
> *omelet piping-hot; item fourth, one half of a rizzard haddock;*
> *add to these home-baked bread in the form of scones and oatcakes,*

My father was a good hand at breakfast, being especially fond of smoked salmon and venison collops at which none alive could match his cook, Kate Archy.

Osgood Mackenzie, *A Hundred Years in the Highlands*

---

as well as honey, marmalade at discretion, plenty of cream and real good coffee, and you will give me credit for having break-fasted. There was a dram afterwards, but that is never counted, although the whisky is well disguised in several tablespoons of heather honey. We started for the seat of war about seven o'clock, mounted [unsurprisingly, it might be thought] on ponies.

But these – breakfast and luncheon – were mere playthings, timid introductions to the manlier pleasures of the after-the-stalk dining-room: and there is no better to introduce them than the mighty Isabella Beeton herself.

This, after all, was Britain at the height of her colonial power, in the balmy days of that great, never-ending imperial summer which would introduce, in its time, great war. The national cuisine had moved far from its fourteenth-century delights of roast heron and baked hedgehog, or the eighteenth-century pleasures of sucking rabbit, venison pasty, and roast teal, quail and snipe.

Certainly, luncheon remained an important ritual in the stalking day, but the food was much more modern. Had stress of weather detained a party from going to the hill, for instance, they might lunch in-lodge and could expect to find on the table: *Fillets of sole in mayonnaise; iced lobster soufflé; braised beef with savoury jelly; dressed ox-tongue; fillets of duckling with goose liver farci; braised stuffed quails; roast pheasant in crust; Japanese salad; border of rice with stewed prunes; cakes; savouries; cheese; and dessert.*

A Beeton luncheon-box – adequate if not specifically for the hill – was no less ambitious. At 1909 prices, a party of twenty could enjoy at a total cost of just under £4 the following: *Four lobsters; ten pounds of beef wing rib; four roast chickens; one small ham; two chaud-froid of chicken; one veal and ham pie; salad and dressing; two fruit tarts; cream; two jellies; four loaves; two pounds of biscuits; one and a half pounds of cheese; half a pound of butter; and a dozen each of pears, bananas and apples.*

Retainers and servants would naturally also bring to the mountain

> *A Lady Perth of olden times met a Frenchman who disparaged Scottish cooking. 'Weel, weel,' observed her ladyship with vernacular asperity, 'some fowk like parritch, and some fowk like puddocks.'*
> Dean Ramsay, *Reminiscences of Scottish Life and Character*

The Fare of Keepers and Kings

> ❦ *Margaret (Meg) Dods, one of the great Scottish cookery writers, was the pseudonym of Mrs Christian Johnston. To her culinary talent she added that of wit. On one occasion she visited the poet James Hogg, who escorted her to the local Fairy Well and handed her a glass of its water with the comment, 'Mrs Johnston, any married woman who drinks a tumbler of this will have twins within a year'. Mrs Johnston promptly replied, 'In that case, Mr Hogg, I shall only take half a tumbler'.*
>
> Sir Walter Scott, *Journal*

appropriate ancillary equipment in the form of wines, mineral waters, lemon juice, plates, dishes, knives, forks, spoons, glasses, tablecloths, napkins, glass-cloths, corkscrews, champagne-opener, castor sugar, oil, vinegar, mustard, pepper, cayenne, salt and pickles.

But still – such luncheons were no match for the rigours of a long day, and it was to the lodge dining-room that the stalkers would direct their attention on their return from the hill.

Naturally enough, dishes of game, of both the flying and walking kinds, figured prominently, and Mrs Beeton offers an unmatched illustration of what might be on offer and of how it might have been cooked. Some of the dishes are perhaps overly sturdy for modern sensibilities, such as black cock, capercaillie, corncrake, bunting, plover and ptarmigan – along with the singularly unsporting dishes of *pâte de merle* and *grive rôtie*.

But it is with the more usual classes of gamebirds, along with venison and salmon, that Mrs Beeton is primarily concerned. And though she can manage just two recipes for grouse, and only nine for venison, she includes no fewer than twenty-four for salmon.

For roasted grouse (*'its flesh is of an exquisite flavour'*) the cook required two birds, two slices of toast, butter, good brown gravy, bread sauce, fried breadcrumbs and bacon.

> *Let the birds hang in a cool, dry place for three or four days. When ready for use, pluck, draw and truss them in the same manner as roast chicken. Tie over each breast a thin slice of bacon, and roast before a clear fire from thirty to thirty-five minutes, basting frequently with butter. When nearly done, remove the bacon, dredge with flour, and baste well to give the birds a nice brown appearance. Toast the bread lightly and, when the*

The Fare of Keepers and Kings

> *The Edwardian period was not afraid to proclaim its status-distinctions. One whisky producer advertised ten-year-old malt Lagavulin Selected at 120p the gallon. The younger blend of Old Highland, however at just 90p the gallon, was advertised as 'suitable for gillies and beaters'.*

birds are about three-quarters cooked, put it into the dripping-tin to catch the gravy that drops from them. Dish on the toast, and serve the gravy, bread sauce and breadcrumbs separately. Cost (of grouse): 20p the brace.

For one of her venison dishes (a modest one by her standards), the required ingredients are one pound of venison, the juice of three small onions, an egg, an ounce of butter, parsley, flour, nutmeg and seasoning.

Pound the peeled, sliced and blanched onions in a mortar until reduced to a pulp, place this in muslin, and press out the juice with the back of a wooden spoon. Remove all skin, fat and gristle from the meat, chop it finely, and mix with it the onion-juice, parsley and a pinch of nutmeg. Stir in the egg, season to taste, form into flat cakes the size and shape of a fillet, and coat them lightly with flour. Heat the butter in a chafing-dish, put in the steaks and fry gently for ten minutes, turning them once. Place the cover on the chafing-dish, continue to cook gently for five minutes longer, then serve. Cost: 10p. Serves: 3 or 4.

But it is when Mrs Beeton comes to fish that the full style – or flavour – of the contemporary kitchen becomes apparent. For *Paupiettes of Salmon Régence Style* the ingredients are listed as two and a half pounds of salmon, one large whiting, three ounces of panada, two ounces of butter, two egg yolks, a spoonful of Béchamel sauce, seasoning, a teaspoon of parsley, preserved mushroom heads for garnish and Régence sauce.

Remove the fillets of salmon from the bone, cut off the skin, divide each fillet in half lengthwise, and cut them into rather thin long slices of even size, trimming them neatly. Skin and bone the whiting, pound it in a mortar until smooth, add the panada, mix well, then add the egg yolks, about one ounce of butter, the Béchamel sauce and the chopped parsley. Season to taste with salt, pepper, cayenne and nutmeg, and rub through a fine sieve.

The Fare of Keepers and Kings

Spread each slice of salmon with a layer of this farci or forcemeat, roll up into paupiette shapes, and tie each with string or skewer them together in twos or threes. Place them in the sauté-pan containing one ounce of melted butter, divide the remainder of the butter into little bits, placing these on the top of the paupiettes, cover with a butter paper, and cook in a moderate oven from twenty to twenty-five minutes, basting frequently. When done, take up, remove the skewers or string, and dress the paupiettes on a hot dish. Have the Régence sauce nicely heated, add the mushroom heads, allowing one large head for each paupiette; place the mushrooms on the paupiettes, and serve hot. Cost: 25p to 30p. Serves: 10.

But such dishes were the stuff of lodge, mansion and castle; they were not, it may be asserted with confidence, the everyday fare of the labouring masses, urban or rural, Scottish or English.

Still, in the Highlands, where the common people claimed access by right of history and culture, if not by alien law, to the produce of moor, mountain and river, game was no stranger to the popular table. The Highlands had their own traditions of popular hunting, which were of somewhat greater antiquity – dignity, indeed – than those of the recreational hunting class.

Poacher's broth, for instance, was as formidable as anything that might appear on the shooting-lodge table (and if it were a lot simpler to cook, its ingredients would not have been quite so simple to catch). In Margaret (Meg) Dods' brisk description, *'this savoury and highly relishing new stew-soup may be made of any or everything known to the name of game'*, and she does not exaggerate.

In her recipe, two to four pounds of venison, a whole blackcock, a pheasant entire, a hare (just a half) and a brace of grouse are boiled with

---

Salmon was once so plentiful that the Highland upper class thought it a foodstuff most suitable for servants. In his *Letters from a Gentleman in the North of Scotland* (1754), Burt tells of a chieftain and his retainer dining in a London tavern. Of the beef he ordered a steak for himself but, 'let Duncan have some salmon'. To be short, the Master's eating was eight pence, and Duncan's came to almost as many shillings.

whatever spices and vegetables are to hand, the lot, should resources permit, and then optionally, coloured with red wine. *'Let the soup simmer until the game is tender, but not overdone; and, lest it should, the vegetables may be put in half an hour before the meat.'*

Slightly more than a century later, Marian McNeill's grouse soup was almost as robust and not much more complicated, requiring *'two old birds'*, celery, peppercorns, juniper berries (optional), salt, cayenne pepper, butter, oatmeal, beef stock, port or red wine, and whisky or cream.

Her salmon soup is equally simple, requiring the trimmings of a fish, the bones of one or two whitings *('these make all the difference')*, carrot, turnip, onion, celery, parsley, breadcrumbs and mashed potatoes.

And when it comes to salmon as a main course, McNeill and Dods *('nothing is more disgusting and unwholesome than underdone fish')* are in agreement on two things: it need not of necessity be fresh, but it should be cooked simply.

Says Dods, *'where the fish is not fresh, and served in what is esteemed by some as the greatest perfection, crisp, curdy and creamy'*, it should be presented with no more than the water in which it is boiled, as sauce. And, she adds, *'Mustard is considered an improvement to salmon when overripe – beginning to spoil, in short; the fish may then be boiled with horse-radish'*.

Meanwhile, McNeill's Tweed Kettle (though doubtless a fish from the Tilt would do the job just as well) contrasts markedly with Beeton's idea of salmon, requiring one (fresh) fish, a handful of spices and vinegar.

> *Cut a pound of fresh salmon, freed from skin and bone, into one-inch cubes. Season with salt, pepper and a tiny pinch of*

Game, to keep from tainting. In cold, frosty weather game may be hung from two to three weeks in an ordinary larder without becoming tainted, but when the atmosphere is warm and damp, great care should be taken to hang it in a well-ventilated place, preferably where there is a current of air. The feathers are a great protection from flies, but it is advisable to apply a good sprinkling of pepper, which usually serves to keep away these pests.

Mrs Beeton, *Household Management*

The Fare of Keepers and Kings

> *A deer would be killed and the venison would be hung up in the spray of a great waterfall which entirely prevented any blue flies getting at it.*
>
> Osgood Mackenzie, *A Hundred Years in the Highlands*

mace, and place in a fish kettle or saucepan with a minced shallot or a tablespoonful of chopped chives. Add half a cup of water and a quarter cup of wine vinegar or white wine, bring to the boil and simmer very gently for about thirty-five minutes. Add a tablespoonful of chopped parsley shortly before dishing up.

In *The Scots Kitchen* McNeill also includes an exceedingly simple way of cooking venison, given her by the daughter of a Highland gamekeeper. No more in the way of ingredients are needed than venison, salt and pepper, flour and bacon fat or beef dripping. The diced meat is dipped in seasoned flour, cooked in two inches of fat until done, and served with flour-thickened gravy.

Of this dish she says, *'This is perhaps the simplest and (say the gillies) certainly the best way of cooking venison, as it completely counteracts the natural dryness of the meat. One or two sliced onions may be browned in the fat before the venison is put in. One or two chopped rashers of bacon may be added. A few chestnuts, peeled and scraped, may be cooked with the meat.'* She concludes drily, *'And the laird adds a glass of port wine'.*

And today food remains an important part of the deer-stalking and grouse-shooting scene.

Yvonne Learmonth, who cooks for Glen Tilt shooting parties at Forest Lodge, offers a plain but very traditional breakfast of porridge – but recognizes that the plainest of foods are often the most difficult to cook well and require the finest of ingredients.

For breakfast she offers the guests porridge made with oatmeal from the Mill at Alford in Aberdeenshire, and which she considers to be the best meal in Scotland. Bacon is home cured, from an exceptionally good butcher in Pitlochry, while eggs are always free-range. Toast is made on the Forest Lodge Aga (the best toast there is, she says) and served with various types of home-made marmalade.

A shooting-lunch could consist of flasks of soup, various filled rolls and a whole cooked ham on the bone, the lot washed down with a generous draught of sloe gin.

Dinner, however, offers a lighter touch than in days gone by. It might

The Fare of Keepers and Kings

> Food has risen in price somewhat since the time of Mrs Beeton. In 1909 a brace of grouse cost from 20p. Nowadays, a brace of grouse in Harrods might cost as much as £40 on 13 August, but the price will fall to as low as £16 later in the season. The ingredients for Mrs Beeton's *Paupiettes of Salmon Régence Style*, serving ten, can no longer be bought for 25p to 30p but will cost £20.19. And her shooting-party buffet luncheon, for twenty Edwardian diners, no longer amounts to just £4; today it would cost £180.09.

open with a starter of fan-cut avocado served with a spinach and garlic mayonnaise and garnished with prawns and a whole langoustine, followed by a soup such as bortsch.

The main course reverts to tradition, and would most likely be of a roast haunch of venison, cooked according to its quality and type. It would be served with redcurrant and rowan jelly; dauphinoise potatoes; roast parsnips; red cabbage with apple; and a gravy flavoured with a little port and redcurrant jelly.

And the sweet too – cranachan – is traditional. As she says, '*Mix a quantity of whipped double cream with half that quantity of cream cheese, and add enough runny honey to sweeten it. Scatter some toasted pinhead oatmeal over the lot, and mix again. Add some whisky and Drambuie, whip, and stiffen the mixture in the fridge. Serve in individual glasses, on a bed of fresh raspberries, which must not be sweetened, and garnished with thin slices of home-made shortbread.*'

And for wine? To taste, she says, but adds, '*Any burgundy or claret goes well with venison: the real secret, for wine or venison, is always to have the best possible quality*'.

MAY

By now, by the time we are into May, we are well into spring, and indeed if it has been a good one you might think – towards the end of the month – that the summer has come round once again. And by now, too, we have a lot of work on our hands, because in the last few weeks the ewes have started lambing, so we not only have to concern ourselves with that but also with guarding the new lambs from the foxes and the crows.

I suppose you could say it all starts with the choice of the tup himself – that's the ram who has covered the breeding ewes the previous autumn, and who is the father of the lambs born the following spring.

Every tup was a lamb himself once, of course, and you could say a lucky one too. He is usually selected by a keen-eyed shepherd who spots his potential, because when the lambs are young they are sorted out into female lambs, which will be kept for producing lambs in the future, and into male lambs.

The male lambs don't have that sort of future to look forward to. A handful in any flock are selected and kept for breeding some time in the future. You might select eight good tup lambs from a flock of maybe three hundred lambs. And the rest get castrated so that some day they will make good mutton for the table: a lot of city folk maybe don't know that that's the way it works, but those are the hard facts of the matter whether you like it or not.

A lamb is selected to be a tup for his looks, his size, breadth of chest – just whatever a shepherd's instinct and experience tell him about the lamb. He is then put aside and probably fed a bit better than the others, maybe hand-fed, before he is sold on to another shepherd, as you don't want him interbreeding with the flock from which he came. Likewise, you have to buy in tup lambs for your own sheep, and you need a keen eye when you go to the tup sales to get them.

When you get them home, you do look after them carefully. After all, without them, there would be no lambs at all in the future. You usually need a few of them to get round all the ewes, which we start taking in for tupping some time around November. Obviously, in low country you can start a lot earlier, which means that they can have lambs around Christmas-time. It is usually about five months less five days from the tupping until the first lambs start to appear.

The ewes come into season over a sixteen to seventeen day period, and it is naturally a busy time for the tups. More often than not they have had some sort of special feeding before they are put to the ewes. Normally, one tup would cover around forty ewes – sometimes as few as twenty, and sometimes as many as fifty – and after that he is pretty worn out and needs careful looking after.

Sometimes a ewe does not come into lamb. We call that one a yeld ewe, though nowadays you have scanning machines which will tell you not only if a ewe is in lamb but whether she is carrying one, two or even three lambs.

If a ewe is yeld, naturally you would tend to feed her less over the winter; though you can often tell a yeld ewe in the spring because, less feeding or not, they still look in pretty good condition, whereas the ewes that have had to carry lambs are feeling the pinch, especially after a hard few months of snow and frost.

And so, in the last week of April and the first days of May, we begin to see the lambs appear, and this is a very tense time for us, and a very busy one too. Personally, I like to start at five in the morning or even a wee bit earlier, because they are my sheep, they are my responsibility, and if I have a dead lamb then that is my fault. You really have to keep an eye on all the ewes at this time, because some of them can have real trouble with the birth – or births, in the case of twins, though you are lucky to have a quarter of the ewes carrying twins. And triplets are very rare.

In any case, you are often better with just one lamb per ewe, because it is likelier to be a big and strong lamb, better able to survive the first few days of life. A single lamb also gets the mother's complete attention, whereas with twins, if there is a shortage of milk, a ewe, especially a young one, might let a lamb slip away.

Even with single lambs, mind you, the odds are stacked pretty high against them. A mother can lamb on a very cold day, for example, or she can give birth into a pool of water, and the lamb might not have the strength to struggle out of it. Still, the mothers are usually very quick to attend to a new lamb, licking it clean at once, and almost as quickly getting it to suckle for milk. Because ewe's milk is a very strong sort, and once a lamb gets a good taste of it, then it is likely to survive – as long as the weather, or the foxes, don't get it.

Snowstorms they can usually survive surprisingly well as long as they don't get covered over. Sometimes the ewe will lie down and give her lamb some shelter from the snow. Indeed, I have seen lambs lying on top of their mothers for warmth.

But the first few hours – you might almost say the very first hour – is crucial for the survival of any lamb. That's why, at the lambing time, I try to keep my ewes well under observation by keeping them in two lambing places in a paddock area, so that I can go out first thing every morning and see what's what. I can see at once if there are any ewes having difficulty lambing. Once a ewe has given birth she can normally look after the lamb on her own, but sometimes a ewe can't give birth naturally. So you have to help it out and get it suckling – because once the mother has smelt the lamb it will stay with her until it is taken away from her.

Mind you, it's not always as simple as that. If a ewe is poorly and doesn't have milk, she will sometimes abandon her lamb. Or say her lamb dies for some reason, the ewe might go and try to steal another sheep's lamb. If that happens, normally we would take a twin from another ewe and give it to the one whose own lamb had died. Sometimes you take the skin of the dead lamb and tie it over the twin so that the sheep will accept its 'new' lamb. And if she still won't accept it, you might have to tether her for a few days and let the new lamb suckle her. And now and again a mother with twins will only look after one of them.

And while all this is going on, it is always in the back of my mind that the grouse are nesting and the fox is still on the go. This is the time of the year when the foxes really go for the lambs. I

*A buzzard on
a telegraph pole
in the glen*

have seen it myself, about one in the morning in the lambing park, there was a fox with a freshly killed lamb at its feet.

And then, of course, sometimes you have to help a ewe with a difficult birth. You can't call out the vet every time for that sort of thing. Although once, come to think of it, a vet turned up out of the blue. It was about the middle of the lambing season and the weather had been dry, which sometimes makes it difficult for the ewe. This is when you need to get your jacket off and your sleeves rolled up, and maybe turn the lamb to make the birth easier. Well, this day I found a ewe lying at the side of the road and I was just starting to help her when I heard voices. There were three or four walkers there, so I carried on with what I was doing when I felt a hand on my shoulder. The next thing I knew, one of these guys was down on his hands and knees and without any hesitation, in an absolutely professional way, lambed the ewe there and then. I thanked him and he said he was a vet – he lambed her as nice as you like, and a good lamb it was too, that one.

These complications happen quite often, especially with twins – sometimes a head gets twisted around and you have to untwist it. And if the worst comes to the worst, sometimes you have to sacrifice the lamb's life in the cause of saving the ewe herself.

So the early part of May has always been a busy time for people with sheep, though I don't know how much longer it will last. The whole practice of keeping sheep on hill-land in the Highlands is under threat. There's a fair bit of money involved. I reckon you need at least a hundred ewes, perhaps more like two hundred, to make the thing worth while in the first place. Remember, a flock contains sheep of different ages, from last year's lambs to the six-year-old ewe. You might sell off the older ewes every year, and every year keep back some of the ewe lambs to replace them in due course. And you always know their ages because you put a brand on their horns with the date, as well as marking them with a sort of paint for identification purposes. You know – you might have red on *your* sheep and I will have blue on *my* sheep. That's the way we know who they belong to.

The old sheep will sell at maybe £15 to £25 each, while the lambs can fetch about the same, though sometimes the price can go as high as £35. If we get £30 for our lambs, we are well pleased with that. And there is also some money from the clip. Some years a fleece can make £3, but at other times it might be as low as 50p. It fluctuates a lot, and nobody ever knows the price the wool will make. You can be clipping some years and losing money by the time you count the cost of whisky and food for the clippers. But the next year you might be seeing £3 a fleece, which could give a man with a hundred ewes a profit on the wool of £200 or more. Usually, it just about breaks even.

And then there are subsidies from the government: you get so much for each sheep. This is really what keeps the farmer in the black rather than the red a lot of the time. I mean, you could be looking at £30 per ewe, so add in another £30 for her lamb, plus the wool, and multiply that by a hundred – but you have a lot of work to do for it, believe me. It doesn't just walk into your bank account. There is the gathering, the clipping, the dipping, the cost of feedstuffs, veterinary bills, and all the hours spent on the hill trying to control the foxes and the crows.

At lambing time in particular, these predators can cause terrible damage to a flock. It's not a nice thing to be going out in the morning and find a lamb from which a crow has ripped the eyes and the tongue, not nice at all. The lamb is still alive, of course – but the only thing you can do is destroy it there and then. The same thing can happen to a ewe if she is lying on the ground and is heavy in lamb or even giving birth: a hoodie can be off with her eyes in no time. The eagle is another predator. I have never seen one take a lamb, though I have heard of it often enough, but I have seen an eagle take a deer calf. To be fair to the eagle, they usually stick to the hares. But in the spring the hares are white, just like the lambs, and a hungry eagle isn't going to worry too much about what he gets his claws into.

And then there are the lambs that get stranded. Sometimes they will see a patch of grass down a cliff-face and will work their way down to it – and then discover that they can't get back up again. Sometimes they can be two or three hundred feet down on a ledge, on a rock-face, and once or twice a year we have to abseil down and rescue them. I have been doing this for fifteen-odd years, and have done it many times – and I have yet to lose a lamb in the process.

Whether sheep are stupid, mind you, is another question. After all, plenty of climbers can get stranded and need to be rescued as well. When you see a sheep wander about in the middle of a busy road you think they are stupid – but then, they are semi-tame animals and fairly used to people being around them. And if you go out in the winter and rattle a bag of food, they will run from half a mile away to get at it. They are also very instinctive weather-wise; they do seem to have a good idea of what the weather is going to do. They will be down in the valley during the day and go up the hill in the evening – unlike the deer, which stay on the hill during the day but come down at night. Every evening you will see the sheep trekking up to an elevated bit of ground, up the side of the hill. Now and again they are caught out – a bit like ourselves, I suppose. I mean, if the snow comes on and the wind gets up, they can take shelter under a rock, or at the back of a wall some-where. They can be buried four and five feet deep – which is when the shepherd has to go out and search for them.

The shepherd with his daughter and his dog

MAY

This is a time that a good dog comes in useful. Indeed, nobody could work a flock of sheep without a decent collie. They are the right hand and the left hand of any shepherd. I must admit this is one of my weaker points: I am not the most professional sheep-dog handler, though I do get there eventually. The dog for sheep is usually a Border collie, and it takes a lot of training. You get two kinds. One is the sort that will run well and work sheep hundreds and hundreds of yards in the distance, maybe gather sheep off an entire hillside for you. And the second kind will work much closer to the sheep, the sort of dog at lambing which will corner a ewe and keep her there until you can get a hold of her.

It is very important that they are properly trained right from the start, from two or three weeks old, though you don't really get into serious training until they are perhaps a year. It depends very much on what sort of stock they have come from. A flock of sheep will get used to a dog after a while, of course; both dog and sheep get a feel for a routine, if you like. A few barks and a few whistles and the sight of the dog will put the sheep on to their usual path and, once they start to move, the dog just has to keep them moving in the right direction. And usually other sheep will join the moving flock. This way one man and a dog can gather sheep off a stretch of hill maybe four miles long by one mile wide.

But you must have a good dog and be able to handle it properly. This is something that gamekeepers sometimes have a little trouble with. I amn't saying they can't do it – some can do it very well indeed. But a keeper only has so much time to work with sheep and sheep-dogs, unlike a full-time shepherd, and that can make things a little more awkward. If you are working with gun-dogs at the grouse, well, that's time you are not working your sheep-dog. A collie doesn't like standing around the butts doing nothing, for instance, so we are sort of handcuffed in terms of the amount of time we are working with it.

Naturally, these dogs are working dogs and are treated as such. There isn't a great deal of room for sentiment, although people do get awfully keen on their dogs. But you have to watch them too. Say you have an old, fat dog in the city which is kept as a companion for an old lady. Well, if that sort of dog disappears one night, it can't do much damage in the town. But in the country – that's a different matter. If dogs get out and get together, they can do terrible damage worrying sheep or slaughtering pheasants. I have actually seen three dogs which had been living wild in the countryside run down and kill a roe-deer.

So these dogs are not pets, not the sort of dog that you sit down at night and clap because it has done nothing all day. Normally, it will have done as much work as you, and is just as tired after a day on the hill – that's maybe the time and the place for a wee clap. Indeed, I would say that most shepherds and keepers have a lot of affection for their dogs, though perhaps they don't show it too much. I personally have a lot of affection for my terriers and labradors. I will talk about them later on – but I'll just say here that though I am always shouting at them I dread to think of any harm coming to them.

Some people let their dogs into the house, but not often with working dogs. Perhaps only when they have an injury of some sort, say a cut paw or whatever, then a dog will be taken in and given a warm at the fire and so on.

The one thing that does get to me is when a dog is old and just not fit for its work any more. Then we try to keep it for as long as possible, keep it as a pet about the place. You can't expect it to go chasing after sheep on the hill, though a lot of them are still interested in keeping an eye on what's going on around the place.

Of course, they have to die some time – and that's why you always want to have a young dog in reserve, trained up and ready to take over from the old one.

Mind you, how much longer dogs will be working sheep on the Scottish hills is anybody's guess. I can't help thinking that the days of hill-sheep farming are numbered, at least in terms of the way it has been in the past. The system at the moment depends on the subsidies, and I don't see them lasting for ever. A farmer will look around and say, well, without a subsidy there's no way I can afford to pay a shepherd – the price he makes for his lambs wouldn't pay a shepherd's wages, far less leave any sort of profit. And on top of the wages there are all the other costs – so I don't see the present system lasting for too much longer. In some places it is happening already – the sheep are being sold off, the shepherds made redundant or given another job as a handyman or planting trees.

Two dogs in the Land-Rover after a day's hard work

But if it is a large estate there probably are full-time foresters anyway, so there might not be a job for the shepherd, even if he was prepared to give up working with sheep. So if the subsidies go, there will be massive changes. Already there are lots of places paying off the shepherds. They are going to be lorry-drivers and things like that. I can think of two or three friends of mine – one of them is going to be a driver for the council, one is retired completely, and one is taking early retirement because of the rheumatism that a lot of shepherds suffer from.

Yes, the future is at the back of everyone's mind, shepherds and keepers. You might not think it is so bad an outlook for keepers – but I amn't so sure about that either. New conservation laws keep coming in, and they could change the nature of the job for ever. It might some day mean the end of traditional stalking – the keeper would be just some sort of conservation officer. I don't think it will happen in my time – at least, I hope not. But in the next fifteen or twenty years something like this is likely, and in a lot of ways I can see the writing on the wall, not just for sheep and shepherds but in the longer term for keepers as well.

Teach Yourself Stalking:
Top Tips for Tilt

If your idea of sporting wear is a garish shell-suit with designer trainers, then stalking – though you'll certainly be able to claim some sort of first – is probably not for you.

For stalking deer, like any other sporting activity, demands the right sort of clothing, appropriate to weather, time of year, and even the natural ground-cover on any given estate.

Of course, in the case of some truly great stalkers, it hardly mattered what they actually wore. The early nineteenth-century poacher Alexander Davidson, for instance, made do with a thin coat and trousers even in the depths of a Grampian winter. But then Davidson had the patience and endurance of Job, for he slept happily on the hillside for seven months of the year and was able to stand stock-still for hours, to his neck in river-water, waiting to spear a salmon; and he brought the same qualities to his deer-stalking.

Later in the same century, however, the legitimate stalker was often particular about what was worn on the hill. Sometimes, even, there was a recognized, and obligatory, estate 'uniform'.

On Atholl, the kilt was *de rigueur* for the professional stalker (and the kilt has not a few advantages on the hill anyway). For some forests, Harris tweeds were considered best, and on Mull a blue, brown and white check was thought to be indistinguishable from rock.

And, as might be expected, Walter Winans, the famous American millionaire shot, had his own ideas about these things: his breeches were cut off above the knee in the style of an Alpine peasant (*'the knee dries as soon as it gets wet'*), and he changed the colours of his clothes in relation to the *'prevailing tint of the season, getting more yellow and red as the autumn advances'*.

None of these notions is irrelevant to the modern-day stalker, who is, nevertheless, likely to be less fanatical in their application. He (or she) should, however, take care to wear jacket and trousers that blend with the general shooting-ground. His boots should be rubber soled, for the chink of metal on rock can alert a deer. Spectacles are bad news: their glint can reveal a stalker's existence and approximate position.

Dry weather can turn very wet, and very suddenly, on the hill; some form of waterproof overalls (as long as they do not squeak) can be carried. The weather can also get much colder with a rapidity that is particularly dangerous in winter. Items of clothing that protect those parts of the body which lose most body heat (head, neck, wrists) should be carried. And visibility can also fail dramatically; in the case of the lone hunter, a compass and map might some day prove their value.

Thus attired, the stalker turns his attention to the rifle (for the sporting use of which he is, of course, properly licensed). It will be a modern high-power multiple-shot weapon, either semi-automatic or bolt-action, depending on preference. It may be equipped with a sling, for carrying it or for steadying a standing or recumbent shot. It may also be equipped with telescopic sights (though some marksmen think these sights impede really fast snap-shooting – aiming and shooting very, very quickly).

The rifle can be camouflaged against glint, and the sights will certainly be zeroed for a favoured range. Above all, the hunter will be skilled and practised in the rifle's use, in terms of safety, accuracy and speed of deployment – safety particularly, for the hills are not always as empty of people as they seem, with shepherds going about their work, and walkers and climbers their leisure.

Thus prepared, the hunter will consider the implications of time of year, first of all in terms of weather – in winter change is faster and more dangerous, daylight hours drastically shorter, and nights and dawns on the hill much colder. Time of year also has a bearing on the nature and location of the stalk. In August the stags will be on the high tops and alone, in September at the rut and relatively oblivious to danger; in winter the hinds will be on low ground in herds.

And so our hunter is now ready for the hill. If accompanied by a professional estate stalker, there is only one rule that matters – do, exactly and at once, without sensation of question or doubt, what you are told.

But for many skilled at the sport, the real thrill is solo hunting, preceded

Shepherds and stalkers, eyes trained to their ground and spying detail at distance, and interpreting it, are constantly fed with a stream of information while traversing the hills, most of which is completely elusive to someone versed in a landscape of concrete.

Michael Wigan, *Stag at Bay*

> *Mac had a man out on another occasion who
> missed a shot at a stag, also lying down. The
> stag, in no whit put out by the shot, rose, shook
> himself, turned round unconcernedly and lay down
> again – rump-on, this time. 'He's laughing at you,'
> solemnly asserted Mac.*
>
> Lea MacNally, *Highland Year*

by a long hike to a likely location for deer at the appropriate time of year (unless the hunter is of the modern stalking type who gets driven to the hill in a tracked buggy).

Certainly it will be very early, for – assuming the hunter has not spent the night on the hill, waiting for dawn at a known location of deer – he will want to be up with the deer at their early-morning feeding time.

He may, or may not, have a dog for company. The dog will assist in tracking any mis-shot deer that might avoid a second killer shot and make an escape (for no hunter worthy of the name abandons a wounded beast to that fate). The dog might be a collie. In any case it will be reliably obedient and trained to silence, as well as intelligent and industrious, with a good nose and great stamina.

In any case, too, both dog and hunter will be more than matches for the long, and surprisingly fast, march into the mountains, interrupted only by an occasional 'spy' with a high-power telescope for deer in the upwind distance ahead.

If he is a very skilled stalker, the hunter may identify the trail of a stag or hind (for they differ in footprint and gait) and follow it; or he will simply march onwards, spying now and again, until he is within range of sighting one or more deer.

Now he might pause for something to eat: a sustaining little packed luncheon, doubtless, for the modern stalker. (The poacher Davidson made do with raw oatmeal rendered into solid cakes and flavoured with whisky. It was of this sort of ancient oatmeal snack that Robert Louis Stevenson so aptly observed: *'It provides a good enough dish for a hungry man, and where there are no means of making fire, or good reasons for not making one, it is the chief stand-by of those who have taken to the heather.'*)

So, appropriately sustained, and perhaps a little liquored, our modern stalker begins to move in on his target (unless it is grazing its way towards him, in which case he will simply take cover and wait for it to come into range).

Teach Yourself Stalking: Top Tips for Tilt

This is the highly skilled stalk itself. In the words of the Stuarts:

It is stealing up to the deer when they are lying or feeding, and is that part of deer-hunting which requires the greatest skill, experience and judgement. The use of the rifle is a subordinate art; for it is of no purpose to shoot well if the hunter does not know where to look for, or how to approach, the deer. For this he must possess a keen eye, much promptitude and vigilance, and a thorough knowledge of the habits of the animal.

Scrope says much the same thing: *'This he cannot do without long practice, close observation, and a thorough knowledge of the ground and habits of the animal.'* The hunter must also, again according to Scrope – and at least in Glen Tilt – be very fit.

As Scrope observes, and not entirely facetiously:

He must be able to run in a stooping position, at a greyhound pace, with his back parallel to the ground, and his face within an inch of it, for miles together. He should take a singular pleasure in threading the seams of a bog, or of gliding down a burn on his stomach; accomplished he should be in skilfully squeezing his clothes after this operation, to make all comfortable. A few weeks' practice in the Tilt will make him quite au fait *with this.*

(Making use of burns has always been an essential method of getting close to the quarry: one aristocratic sportsman, the brother of Lord Elgin, was once outraged by a stalker's order to crawl *up* a waterfall.)

> *To my mind, for an outdoor servant, there is no more delightful occupation than that of a deer-stalker. His life is generally spent in wild and magnificent scenery, and though the house or lodge he lives in may be isolated – perhaps twenty miles from the nearest town or village – yet there is a charm in the isolation, and there is a slight romance in living out of the world far from human ken. What can be more delightful than to feel that the 'wild red deer', as they call them, are your only neighbours for miles and miles.*
>
> A. S. Walker and P. J. Mackie, *The Keeper's Book*

The hunter must also make expert use of such cover as is available – which is not always much – whether heather, rocks, scrub or bracken; and to do so in snow, sleet, rain or blistering frost; happy, or at least willing, to be bitten alive by midgies; and alert always to the danger of startling a grouse, or a sheep, or a wild bird, whose alarm-call might alert the deer to his proximity and even position.

Above all he must never, ever, show so much as the top of his head on any skyline. And he must never, absolutely never, be upwind of the quarry (and in very mountainous country must take care that a swirling eddy does not alert the prospective target to his existence).

If the target is alerted, the hunter's task is more than doubly difficult. MacNally beautifully describes in *Highland Year* how hinds betray their nervousness:

> One then lies in a petrified state, torn between hope and despair, spiced, I am afraid, with vindictive rage towards the persistent nosiness of your discoverer; while she, with that mincing, high-stepping, walking-on-hot-coals gait of suspicions unconfirmed, with back of rigid straightness, now retreats, now advances, alerting all the herd by her demeanour, and, to make matters worse, gives vent at intervals to that most uncompromising of all sounds to a stalker's ears, the harsh coughing bark of red deer alarm.

But with luck the hunter can still inch towards the beasts and calculate range, cross-wind effect and whether he is shooting on the level, uphill or down. Should there be a selection of targets, he will choose his with care: if culling hinds, an ill or an old one, if looking for a trophy, the best-looking stag; and he will calculate always the likelihood of getting close enough to his favoured quarry.

The hunter will already have a favoured form of shooting, which is, unless he is very expert, from a prone position, with the barrel lying on some convenient rest, and at a stationary target – only the very best of shots will shoot standing and at a running target.

He will also know that, for very many riflemen, to shoot downhill is to shoot high – that is, to shoot *above* the target. The story is still told of how, on one estate, a 'rifle' repeatedly missed a stag at close downhill range. After every shot, the beast would run fifty yards to a burn, and then run back to his original spot. After the 'rifle' missed for the eleventh time, the professional stalker in his company rose without a word of reproach, put his hands comfortably into his pockets, and sat down on a large boulder on the skyline. Stag and stalker looked at each other with

Teach Yourself Stalking: Top Tips for Tilt

> Be suspicious of too long a 'spy' on the part of
> the stalker – it may only be his lazy way of
> passing the time. Once I caught two stalkers (who did
> not think I understood any Gaelic) 'spying' the oats
> in each other's crofts, and comparing their ripeness,
> when they were supposed to be spying for deer.
>
> Walter Winans, *The Sporting Rifle*

expressionless wonder, and then the stag turned, walked with great deliberation to the edge of the hill, and slowly disappeared.

The huntsman will be ready, too, for an instant reload, if his weapon is not semi-automatic, in case he mis-shoots and a wounded deer begins to make an escape. He will also have his favoured spot at which to shoot, whether head, heart or shoulder.

This is a subject on which Winans had strong views – on which, indeed, many still have strong and conflicting views. In Winans' opinion, *'The best spot to hit is the shoulder, well forward, and not the heart. The stag's heart is perhaps three inches in diameter'* – which was, for Winans, with his preference for running targets, *'an uncertain mark to hit in a galloping beast at long range. The shoulder offers a far larger mark in the first place. And secondly, a stag hit in the shoulder by a solid bullet, or one which does not expand too rapidly, drops at once and is done with.'*

The hunter's last enemy is buck-fever, that trembling fear which comes over amateur shots at the very point of squeezing the trigger of their rifle.

Augustus Grimble recognized it thus:

The disease must run its course. Advice will not cure it, neither will whisky; but after a course of downright bad misses the foresight of your rifle will by degrees cease to wobble round and round. The eye will see clearly that there is a stag within a hundred yards, and the brain begin to tell that it will be better to keep the sight steady if you wish to taste one of his haunches instead of sending him off to give a treat to a neighbour.

And the condition is still encountered today. Says Charlie Pirie:

You come across so many laid-back guys who just want to shoot a stag. They have all the right gear – guns, waterproofs, binoculars and so on – but when you get within a hundred yards of the kill,

99

they start to get the fever, the stag-fever. Even guys who come year in, year out, experienced hunters, no difference, they get the fever, and, my God, do some of them get it bad!

He adds:

I take the shooting party up on a stalk. It could take us a whole day to get in a position to shoot. We may have lain in the wet heather in the pouring rain for hours, sometimes crawling a few inches every few minutes. We could have walked miles up and down the peat hags in half a gale. We get exhausted. And then the opportunity to stalk the last few yards arrives. The magnificent sight of the beasts wipes out all thoughts of tiredness. I hand the gun to the guest and I get him into position, and always give them a second glance to check for the fever. I can feel it before I see it; I swear sometimes I can smell it too. And then it starts: first the heart pounding, boom, boom, boom, getting quicker and louder, then the tell-tale switch of the gun followed rapidly by hand-shake, sweat and the occasional breathless grunt. If I don't catch them in time, the shaking trigger finger snaps back, the explosion echoes off the surrounding hills, and a startled or injured stag takes to his heels.

But if the first shot is an evident success, and the hunter does not desire to try for a second kill, he will move very carefully on the dead beast, for on occasions a presumed kill has been alive and able to turn on the hunter with potentially dangerous consequences.

Having ensured that it is indeed stone-dead, the true hunter will then begin the dirty – arguably loathsome – process of bleeding and gralloching the kill: that is, cutting its throat (if intended for human consumption) and disembowelling it – with regard to which there is one key lesson, which will never need to be repeated: do not burst open with the gutting knife the intestinal bag of the beast!

And so ends the easy part of the day: finding, killing and preparing for transport the quarry. The modern solo stalker – newspaper editor, venture capitalist or whatever, with the help, perhaps, of his mobile telephone – will call for estate support to remove the carcass by pony or Snocat.

In earlier times, of course, stalkers were built of sturdier stuff: they would sling the beast over their shoulders and carry it home themselves.

❧ JUNE ❧

By June we are well into the summer: long days, short nights, and with a bit of luck some good weather for a while. Usually, everything is under control at this time of the year. The lambs are coming on, we are keeping an eye on the grouse and hoping for a good season, the deer are away in the hills and fish are running in the Tilt and it's the time of the year for poachers to be out and about too.

Not that we are bothered too much with poachers up the glen. There's just the one road, and it is easy to watch – people are so damn lazy nowadays they won't shift out of their own way unless they have a car to do it for them.

But still, salmon and sea-trout are always like a magnet to poachers, whether in this district or anywhere else in the Highlands. There are commercial poachers and there are the old style of 'one-for-the-pot' poachers. I think I have caught people who have taken one for the pot. It is probably more embarrassing for me to catch them than for them to be caught: they don't like to be caught, but I can't say I like catching them. But if you find them at it red-handed, you can't very well ignore it.

I mean, if it is someone who just takes the odd fish now and again that's not so bad, but sometimes you'll get someone going over the score and trying to make a big thing out of it. Well, then it's only a matter of time until they get caught and they have only themselves to blame. In the estate we take a very dim view of that sort of behaviour.

There are any number of ways of taking a fish, of course. One way is a snicker, usually a treble hook with a big lump of lead tied on to it. You drop it into a pool and just pull it backwards and forwards for a while until the hook falls into a fish and you drag it

Waterfall near
Forest Lodge

up on to the bank. It could be foul-hooked anywhere: in the belly, in the tail, or whatever. This does a lot of damage to the fish, naturally, though I suppose if you just want it to eat it doesn't matter too much one way or the other.

Some poachers – definitely of the commercial variety – will use various sorts of poisons, various sorts of materials that are very easy to come by if you know what they are. These things will take

the oxygen out of the water and kill the fish. The poacher will put it in at the top of a pool and as the stream runs down so will the poison, and it will kill fish for maybe two hundred yards downstream, or even more. So then the poachers just collect them and stick them into bags – they are quite safe to eat. When they have got as much as they can carry, they just leave what is left and that can be another two hundred yards of dead fish floating down the river for miles. It is a horrible way to kill fish, and a terrible waste of them. You would never catch what you might call a 'proper' poacher doing this.

But the snicker is a bit more respectable. I am sure many old-style poachers – maybe even a keeper now and again – have been known to try their hand at it. You creep down to the side of the pool, spot your fish and snicker it – it's not so difficult if you know how.

But there are many other ways to take a fish too: nets, otters, gaffs, explosives, fancy baits like prawns, guddling and so on.

The otter is more of a thing for use in still water like a loch, though I suppose you could also use it on a quiet and wide stretch of a river. It's just a board on the end of a long line. Off this line are a lot of droppers, each armed with a hook. As you walk slowly up the bank towing the board it swims away from you and you pay out the line until eventually you are trailing maybe fifty hooks across the stretch of water. I have heard it said that in the right place they are pretty deadly – which is why they are illegal, of course.

A gaff is a big hooked piece of metal, and it can be used in two ways. It can be used at night with a flashlight. You go down to the edge of the river and put the light on the water and fish will swim towards it. You just lower the gaff gently underneath it and grab it out: though if it is a big fish you might want a barb on the gaff and a piece of cord from the handle of the gaff tied to a tree, or something like that. Because if the fish is big and strong enough, you could take a while to land him – if he doesn't pull you into the water first of all!

Some people are also pretty good with the snare; you just take a normal rabbit snare – but it needs a lot of skill to use it with any success. Depending on the depth of the water, it can be hand-held or it can go on the end of a fishing-rod. On a nice sunny afternoon, the fish can be seen easily lying in a pool, so you drop the snare down into the water and bring it along very slowly and quietly until it goes over the tail of the fish. Sometimes the fish takes off, so again you need a very, very strong line to hold it, though it doesn't take long for the fish to tire and you just pull it out on to the bank.

Gill nets are another way of taking a fish. You string a net across the top of the pool and then throw stones into the bottom end of the pool, and try to drive the fish up into the net – you will never drive fish downstream with stones. This is a very popular method, and sometimes the poachers might clean out the whole pool, except perhaps for the odd fellow tucked right in under the bank. If it is done in the dark, then the fish won't see the net, and there's no chance of them looking for some corner to sneak past it. But if it is daylight, you must make sure that there is no room for the fish to see a way past the net. Sometimes, they tell me, the fish just won't go near the net if they can see it – so then your poacher will sweep the pool with it and draw it up into a smaller and smaller bag which you haul out on to the bank, hopefully full of fish.

Another way is using explosives, though they are very hard to come by nowadays compared to, say, twenty-odd years ago. You just throw a stick into the water, the fish are stunned and float to the top, and you simply collect them as they float down on the stream.

Of course, you can also poach with a rod and line, though you might also use methods that are not necessarily legal or sporting. Prawns, for instance, are very good on a hook at the end of a rod and line, or so I have heard it said, anyway. Mind you, there are deadlier baits than prawns. In fact, I have also seen a salmon shot – the fish was swimming along the surface of this pool, and the man who had the rifle just lifted it over the top of the bridge and put a bullet straight through the fish. That was a very clean and effective way of taking the salmon.

There is an old story to the effect that one of the dukes in days gone by told a keeper that he was having a dinner-party the next night and could do with a nice six-pound salmon for it. 'Very good, Your Grace,' says the keeper. And the next evening there was a lovely six-pound salmon on the duke's dinner-table. Well, you can't fish to size with a rod and line, so you can imagine how that salmon came to be on the duke's table.

Of course, there's also guddling, which is a thing I think every Scottish schoolboy has tried his hand at once or twice. Basically, you lie down at the edge of a burn and put your hands very slowly under the bank, very slowly put them under a fish and get hold of

Loch Moraig

it at the gills and the tail, and whip it out on to the bank. It's not as easy as it sounds – they are slimy and slippery and it is easy to let them slip out of your hands. So when you seize it, the trick is to at once roll over on to your back and slip the fish up over your head with an over-arm movement: that's one more way of taking a fish.

It would be daft to say that there isn't a romantic side to poaching, because there is. Indeed, there have been a few great poachers in this district over the years, and some of their stories were pretty romantic. There was one called Farquharson, maybe a hundred or a hundred and fifty years ago now. His method was always to walk the marches – that is, the borders of each estate. That way nobody paid any attention to him: if we saw him, we would think he was just over the border of the estate on someone else's land, and vice versa. People would see him and just wave and cry, 'Good morning', thinking he wasn't on their land but just over the march of it. He did this for years and years and, if he was poaching deer, he was strong enough to carry the carcass home on his back. He was very interested in rifles and was a very good shot. Indeed, he invented an action on a rifle called the Farquharson lock, and it is still used today in long-range shooting.

He wasn't just a poacher; he obviously loved the countryside as well. He was in the district and Forest Lodge, that was his area. He would have known the ground better than many of the keepers themselves because he was out there poaching on it so much. In a way he was a real sportsman – he would go out there on the hill for a fine day's sport.

But a lot of deer-poaching isn't so sporting as it was for the likes of Farquharson. Usually they have a van and a spotlight, and blast away at the beasts from the roadside. Or they will leave a man at a place where they know the deer will come down to when it is dark. He will pop off four or five, as many as he can bring down, and then his mates will come by and pick him and the beasts up. These sort of folks usually come from the south of Scotland, maybe even the north of England – and they have nothing at all in common with the sporting one-for-the-pot sort of poacher: for them, it is venison today and breaking into houses tomorrow.

We do our best to stop this sort of slaughter. And we have more eyes and ears than you might think – a lot of the regular drivers on the main roads in winter are clued up, and they will often let us know if something is going on.

But with the ordinary chap it is a different matter – the kind of guy who comes out now and again and gets a salmon from the river or a hind from the hillside or whatever it is he wants. If you know he has done it, you can say, well, don't do it again, or don't make a habit of it, and he will maybe appreciate that. And he will maybe do you a favour later on – so it can work both ways, the relationship between the occasional small-scale poacher and the keeper.

I mean, the kind of guy who takes the occasional pheasant isn't going to cause too much trouble for anyone. They can point a small-calibre rifle with a silencer out of the car window on a Sunday morning when the keeper is having a lie in. You can hear a bang, or the hiss of a silenced .22 – that's the way it is. It doesn't have to be an ordinary firearm either. I can think of one gun I have heard of. It looks like a walking-stick, but when you turn a handle and pull it back you can put a four-ten cartridge into it. When you close it, you turn the handle round further and out pops a trigger. This sort of small-calibre weapon is very handy for a poacher on ducks at short range. After a few hours ducks get used to someone's presence and begin to swim closer and closer – until they are in range of the walking-stick, and that's them on the road to the cooking-pot.

You can get grouse the same sort of ways too. In the early morning in August, and sometimes through the spring, you will get the birds coming down to the roadside to eat some grit – that helps them break up and digest their normal foods. If there is a dyke, the old cock will sit up there and survey the countryside, and then call the family to come in and get some of the grit. Well, that is an enticement for any poacher – he can just cruise along in his car, with the snout of the rifle or gun poking out from the window. A cock grouse twenty or fifty yards away on the top of a wall is a good target. So, bang! – down he goes and into the bag.

This kind of poacher will maybe cruise three or four glens in the early morning, perhaps set off at five on a Sunday, and maybe end up with six brace and that is good fun for him. Likewise, he can do the same with rabbits and hares, or cock pheasants. The Sunday morning is very popular for this kind of thing, because the keeper, the factor, the farmer, tend to be in bed having a lie in. Some conscientious keepers know all about it, though; they are on the ball and out to catch these guys. Sometimes you do and sometimes you don't, and that's fair enough. You win some and you lose some.

Of course, you can also take birds with a snare. Indeed, you can try for roe-deer with the snare as well, not to mention hares and foxes. There are basically two types, the free-run and the self-locking. The self-lockers were very effective for vermin, but we no longer use them: you had to be very careful about where they were set in case they get hold of the wrong thing. The ones we use now for foxes are legal, of course, a sort of steel wire with a loop on the end of it. They have a catch which you can either put around another piece of wire or tie to the bottom of a tree. It is a very good method of taking foxes. It works twenty-four hours a day for you – but if it gets into the wrong hands it can be fatal for a lot of things beyond foxes.

The commercial lot couldn't be bothered with snares, generally – that's a tool for a skilled man, if it is to be used as it should be used.

And to be honest, a lot of the ordinary one-for-the-pot poachers are pretty skilled at the job. I mean, that sort of poacher in a lot of ways is a sort of sportsman, he likes to get his excitement this way in particular. He would not pay for a day's legal sport, not because he can't, but because it wouldn't give him the same fun.

That's what I would call a real poacher – a guy who does it for the sport and not for the money or anything like that.

The Statistical Accounts
of Scotland

In the last decade of the eighteenth century the Highland landowner Sir John Sinclair arranged for the publication of *The Statistical Account of Scotland* (now known as the 'Old'. or 'First' to differentiate it from later accounts). The twenty-one volumes of the *Account* contain a description of every parish in Scotland, each written by the parish minister. An updated version on similar lines, *The New Statistical Account of Scotland*, was published between 1834 and 1845. *The Third Statistical Account* appeared in the years after the Second World War. The culture of modern Scotland can still boast of many monuments to the parish, its guardians and their works; but none, perhaps, is greater or more enduring than these *Accounts*.

Old Atholl: the ministers' reports

These parishes commonly go by the name of the united parishes of Blair-Atholl, and Strowan. Blair (Blàr) properly signifies a plain clear of woods; but as the Celts, of whom the Gaels were a branch, in general chose such plains for their fields of battle, Blàr came at length to signify a battle.

The ancient Celtic names of places and things were generally short descriptions of them, though in some cases they originated from remarkable persons and accidental circumstances. It is the more necessary to ascertain these derivations now as the country historians, who in general can best account for these things, are daily growing worse. No time, therefore, should be lost in collecting what information yet remains before it is entirely gone, perhaps never to be recovered.

These united parishes are situated in the shire of Perth, in the presbytery of Dunkeld, and the synod of Perth and Stirling. Their extent is upwards of thirty miles in length; and above eighteen miles in breadth. On the summits of the high mountains, the weather has left little else but gravel and stones, covered with moss.

Lower down is heath, peat-bog, vales full of pretty good pasture, and here and there a green spot, with huts upon them; to which the women, children and herds retire with the cattle for the summer season. In the sides of the glens

111

and valleys the soil is various; in several places it is thin and light, as it is also in the bottoms where the rivers once ran; in other places it is good.

In the summer season the face of the country is green, with corn, grass and wood. In the bottom of every glen and valley, there is a river or stream; and in some of them a loch, or lake. The rest of the parish consists of many glens that fall from the mountains, and of rocks, and extensive hills; of which very little more is capable of cultivation.

There are many considerable mountains; the most remarkable of them are Beinn-deirg, which rises 3550 feet above the level of the sea, and Beinn-glo, the highest pinnacle of which, Carn-nan-gour, rises 3724 feet above the said level.

Strath-dhrnaidh, in Struth-groy, is one of those roundish green hills, that they call the hill of peace, because on these they made peace, and other contracts, of old. They probably reckoned the matters here transacted the more solemn too, as they believed that the fairies, supposed to dwell in these hills, to be witnesses of their transactions.

There are many lochs and two considerable rivers in the parish. Salmon come up the Tummel to the Fall, but the arts that are now practised by the fishers below, let very few salmon the length of either river.

Though it cannot be exactly determined, the probability is that the number of people in the parish is diminished, owing to several causes. When people of small landed property no longer lived upon the produce of their estate, but followed the example of their wealthier neighbours, in the use of foreign commodities, they contracted debt, sold their estate, and went to pursue their luck elsewhere.

When men of landed property could no longer make their tenants fight their battles, they became less careful of having clever fellows about them, and so began to consider how they might make the most of that class of men in another way. Then the rents began to be raised, the farms to be enlarged, much land to

The number of mechanics is,

Smiths	6	Shoemakers	9
Carpenters	27	Flax dressers	16
Weavers	38	Masons	3
Tailors	32	Midwives	2

Physician, surgeon or attorney, there is none.

The Old Statistical Account

> *Ride eastward over a hill into Glen Tilt, famous
> in olden times for producing the most hardy
> warriors; it is a narrow glen, several miles in length,
> bounded on each side by mountains of an amazing
> height. Ascend a steep hill and find ourselves on an
> Arrie, or tract of mountain which the families of one
> or two hamlets retire to with their flocks for pasture in
> summer. Here, we refreshed ourselves with some goats'
> whey, at a* Sheelin *or* Bothay, *a cottage made of turf,
> the dairy house, where the Highland shepherds, or
> graziers, live with their herds and flocks, and during
> the fine season make butter and cheese.*
>
> Thomas Pennant, *Tour in Scotland,* 1771

*be taken into the landlord's domain, and the shepherd and his dog to be the
inhabitants of farms that formerly maintained many families; though this
last particular is not, as yet, so much the case here as it is in many other
places.*

*In consequence of these changes, some of the tenants have become cottagers;
some have removed to the towns, to gain a livelihood by labour; and a few have
emigrated to America, though that spirit has not become very common here
as yet.*

*There are at present only eleven heritors, one of whom (the Duke of Atholl)
possesses at least one half of the parish. Five of these, either occasionally, or
constantly, reside in it.*

*The most common vices here are such as may be expected in that state of
society where the people are poor and where the most extensive farmers have
but little to themselves after paying the landlord. They have a reasonable share
of acuteness, are disposed to be friendly to each other, hospitable to strangers,
and charitable to the poor.*

*The gentlemen are tall and handsome and fond of a military life; and,
though the common people have learnt to despise a soldier's pay, and to hate a
life of servitude, yet there is still a deal of the martial spirit remaining; and
make very good soldiers, when once they undertake it; being firm, hardy and
brave, though not generally tall.*

*Seven or eight hundred of them attended the Marquis of Montrose till after
the battle of Kilsyth, and distinguished themselves by their fidelity and valour.*

The Gaelic language is spoken here by the natives; and there are but few others in the parish. It was in all probability the first language spoken in this country; that it gave the names to places is clear.

The name of the country Atholl (or Adh-oll) is evidently from this source. Adh signifies pleasantness, and oll, great: great pleasantness; Beinn-glo, the mountain with the veil (of clouds and snow); Beinn-deirg, the red mountain, on account of the red granite in it; Beinn-vu-rich, the hill of the rutting.

The names of the rivers too are from the same language; Garry (Gath-ruith), the flight of the dart, because of its rapidity; Tummel (Taivil), shadowy, from its wooded sides; and Tilt (Te-alt), the warm river, from its sheltered banks.

Adapted from the report of the Rev. James MacLagan
in *The Old Statistical Account,* 1791

The climate is dry which may be inferred from the central situation of the country, it being equidistant from the German and Atlantic oceans. Rain comes with an east or south-east wind which, on account of the intervening hills, loses much of its humidity before it reaches the vale of the Garry.

The climate is also cold, which its elevation must indicate. The north wind blows with piercing keenness; and frosty dews are frequent in the beginning of summer and in autumn. The great age to which many of the people live attests, however, that the climate is salubrious. The oldest man in the parish at present is ninety-seven years of age.

Atholl Forest is a mountainous tract of land furnished solely with deer and other game. Its extent and superiority to every other forest are well known.

The jay and the woodpecker are to be met with in the plantations of Blair. The land-rail, the cuckoo, and the swallow, the woodcock and the fieldfare, are our migratory birds, and visit the country in their season.

Blair Castle is the baronial mansion of the Atholl family. It is a building of great strength, magnitude and extent. The date of its erection is not known. It is generally supposed to have been built by John of Strathbogie, a Cumin, who became Earl of Atholl in right of his wife. A part of the castle is still known as Cumin Tower.

Its locality rendered it an important military post in the warfare of feudal times; and in 1750, two storeys were taken from its height, and the great military garrison of the country converted into a modern building. Its apartments are numerous and elegant, and its accommodations are suited to the residence of a ducal family.

The park contains many hundred acres of excellent arable land, exclusive of its extensive plantations; the garden is large and productive; the gravel walks along the Tilt, the Banavy, the Fendar, the Bruar, and the Garry all afford the advantage of active exercise, with the pleasure of admiring mag-

The Statistical Accounts of Scotland

nificent scenery; and, if the whole be viewed in connection with the forest and its lodges, its lakes and its rivers, Blair may be justly said to be one of the most splendid hunting châteaux in Europe.

The gradual decrease of the population is easily accounted for. In former times the higher grounds were inhabited by numerous tenants. Their possessions were small; their supply of food was precarious; and in the very best seasons afforded but a scanty subsistence.

A system of more beneficial management has converted these dreary and comfortless habitations into sheep-walks; and greatly to their own interest, though not perhaps at first so congenially to their feelings, the people have emigrated to the large towns of the south or to America. And though the population upon the whole has diminished, it has greatly increased in the strath of the country, which is certainly a more natural and suitable residence for man than the bleak unsheltered wastes of the mountains.

The people of the country are of middle stature, active and capable of enduring much fatigue. Their food is plain and wholesome; and the poor cottar has his cow, which supplies his family with milk.

The Gaelic is the language of the country. There are few, however, under

---

Glen Tilt, or what is now called the forest by that name, was stated in evidence by the late proprietor – so-called – as covering 100 000 acres. This lovely and fertile strath formerly maintained some 800 of a population; but the people were evicted because they would not compel their youth to enlist in the Atholl volunteers, a fencible regiment designed for seven years' service at home, and to be thereafter disposed of to the East India Company, by which corporation the regiment numbered the seventy-seventh was regularly purchased. Over and above the stock kept in Glen Tilt at present, which is one of the most fertile pasturages in Britain, a large stock of cattle and sheep could be fattened for markets in the south; the exact number it would be somewhat difficult to name, but farmers in the north maintain that Glen Tilt could graze a stock of 90 000 sheep over and above its present number.

Witness to the Napier Royal Commission, 1883, set up to investigate 'the condition of the crofters and cottars in the Highlands and Islands of Scotland'

115

thirty years of age who cannot read, write and speak the English language. The manners of the people, as well as their dress, resemble those of their low-country neighbours, and no power can resist the assimilation of their language.

The elementary books now in Gaelic, and the numerous publications of the present day in that language, whether well or ill executed, and the more general reading of Gaelic in the schools, are but indirect methods of enabling the children to acquire a knowledge of English with greater facility.

Exertions are also made here and there to restore the tartan costume, and the practice of Highland games. Interest and industrious habits render the people indifferent to the latter; and their dress is now regulated by views of comfort and convenience, rather than by vanity or conceit.

The illicit distillation of whisky, which some years ago prevailed in the country, might then have been said to have been a necessary evil. A wiser and more favourable system of excise laws has enabled the Highlander now to convert his barley into money, and to abandon a practice which has well-nigh ruined the country and its people.

If a young man be occasionally found in our distant and extensive moors with a gun in his hand, it need not be wondered at. Sportsmen from the south train them either as servants, or guides, and when their masters leave off their sport, it is not easy for them to relinquish. Poaching, however, is not so general now as it was, and it is getting every year into greater disrepute.

Several important changes in various respects have taken place since the last Statistical Account was written. The great military road from Dunkeld to the north was formed about fourteen years ago into a toll road, which is kept in the very best state of repair. A good road across Sliabh-bac would be highly beneficial, and would facilitate an intercourse with the southern district of the country.

In their dress, as well as in their domestic economy, the people exhibit a very favourable change. In the houses of the peasantry, there is a much greater attention paid to the simple comforts of life. Schools are more numerous, newspapers are abundant, and general knowledge is more widely diffused.

The greatest disadvantage under which this extensive parish labours is the want of divine service every Sabbath day in both its churches. The imperfect system of occasional public worship is the greatest evil and defect – it holds out every encouragement to ignorant and wandering sectarian preachers, or it is apt to confirm a people in habits of indifference to the habitations of religion.

Adapted from the report of the Rev. John Stewart
in *The New Statistical Account*, 1845

❧ JULY ❧

Come July we are all getting ready for the opening of the grouse season next month, which means that all the guns and so on have to be in tip-top condition. Guns and rifles are things I have been around since I was a boy, mind you, and I learnt very early on that they should always be kept in that sort of condition. Fishing-rods and things like that I have never really cared for, but guns and rifles have always been close to my heart, and now I have a bit of a collection of guns. It's not a collection that is just for display, mind you; every one of them has some purpose or another, whether it be for clay pigeons, vermin control or game-shooting. Different jobs, different guns. For instance, if you were teaching a young boy or a lady, you would probably start with a twenty-bore semi-automatic, which means you don't have to keep breaking open the gun to eject the empty cartridge cases.

There isn't a kick off these sort of guns, either, because they are gas-operated. The kick – the recoil – is something that frightens a lot of people starting out shooting, but this isn't a problem with the gas-operated firearm.

They are good for the clays, which is a great pastime, whether you are just learning the sport or have been doing it for years and years. It is also very good practice for when you come to shooting birds and beasts: it develops hand–eye co-ordination for a start, so you learn to shoot clean and correctly from the word go. After all, if you are shooting animals it is very important to be able to do a clean kill. You don't like seeing things running about with broken legs and shot-off wings, for example.

But, again, it is important to be using the right weapon for the job. For every lock there is one key – and that's the way it is with

View of Glen Fender

guns and rifles. If you are deer-stalking you would obviously want a high-velocity rifle with a good telescopic sight. A century ago they would be using old muzzle-loaders with open sights; it's no wonder they needed dogs to go after wounded deer and bring them to bay where they could be killed. But today the rifles are very good indeed and so are the telescopic sights, so there really isn't any excuse for missing a shot.

I suppose it is fair to say that some people have more natural talent than others, but practice improves everyone – though they still must have the right gear. I would always advise someone to buy the best kit they can afford, and I find that a lot of people are willing to listen to what I have to say. I mean, it's part of my job to know these things. A twelve-bore gun with a certain type of cartridge is ideal for pheasants and grouse, maybe another sort of weapon or ammunition for hares, and still another sort for deer. For small ground-game, for instance, you might want to be looking at a light .22 rifle – but you wouldn't use that for deer, of course.

I have examples of most sorts in my collection. I have something like twenty shotguns and six or seven rifles, along with four or five pistols, and I like to think that I am fairly good with all of them.

The most difficult shooting, by the way, is target-shooting with a pistol. Without doubt this is the hardest of the lot, to hit a three-inch bull at twenty-five metres with a handgun. There are any number of makes, and most people have their favourite, but you usually have to try your hand with quite a number before you find the one that suits you best.

It's the same way with guns too, though price certainly is an important factor here. A really top-class pair of guns might cost you £50 000 – not the sort of weapons a gamekeeper can expect to get his hands on! But you can go down to your local gun shop and buy a very nice twelve-bore for £500, and you could expect a second-hand one for around half of that. A single-barrel used gun you could pick up for maybe £100.

Ammunition is another thing you need to consider. If you are shooting large geese you want heavy buck-shot which can penetrate the target properly. But if you are shooting clays you want a small sort of shot but plenty of it. For ground-game like rabbits you would be looking at another sort of shot, or maybe use a light rifle. For shooting something larger like a fox or a deer it is an absolute must to have a rifle of the correct calibre, though gamekeepers can usually take down the target with any sort of weapon.

For deer and foxes you must also have the right sort of telescope. A stalker has to find a herd of deer that may be as far away as five or six miles, and he has to able to tell if he can see a stag in that group and if it is a shootable stag. Otherwise, he might travel all that way to find that there is nothing to shoot.

Of course, people have different ideas of what is the best gear to use. Every time I meet a group of gamekeepers they all have their own ideas, and you will never convince them of anything else. They all have their own convictions – and they are all correct too, because each guy knows what he can do best with each rifle and piece of kit that he has.

They are experts, you could say, and they can handle any type of gun and know when to use it and when not to use it. I mean, a big, strong sort of man who goes out wildfowling and shooting geese will be using a very heavy shot in the gun. For pheasants and duck it would be a lot lighter; or then again you could use a single ball in the shotgun. In some countries this is quite popular, though it doesn't go anything like as far as a rifle. But at short range it can be very effective on large animals.

Now to shoot a white hare we would use a smaller amount of pellets, say a Number Four or Number Five shot, which would be slightly bigger than a Number Seven, but there would be less pellets. It all depends on the nature of the target, and the distance away that it is. Normally, you wouldn't really want to use a gun on anything closer than twenty-five yards or further away than forty yards. Nearer than that and you are liable to put so many pellets into the bird or rabbit that you wouldn't be able to eat it; further away and you might only injure it.

For a fox we might expect to be shooting at thirty yards with heavy BB shot which has about eighty pellets propelled out of the gun by high-velocity powder.

But normally you would want to be using a rifle for any larger-sized sort of animal. OK, the rifle only fires one bullet, but the inside of the barrel has a twist in it – the rifling – which means the bullet is spinning when it leaves the muzzle. This is what gives it speed – over three thousand feet per second – and stability, which mean range and accuracy. It means that over a certain distance the trajectory is completely flat – the bullet does not fall at all. This is what is meant as point-blank range, by the way. Otherwise, of course, you have to zero the rifle for a given range; that is, set the sights so that you aim high to compensate for the fall in trajectory. Usually, the bullet might fall four inches over three hundred yards, that sort of thing. It is a complicated matter, really – a lot depends on the actual weight of the bullet, on the explosive power behind it, and on the length of the rifle barrel.

The important thing is that when the bullet gets to the target it has enough speed and power to punch its way through and kill the beast efficiently, cleanly and at once. This is where the larger-calibre rifles come into their own. It really pays to have a high calibre, because that way you know you are going to penetrate the beast and drop it right there, or very shortly afterwards. You want to hit the beast in the right spot every time, whether that is a neck shot or a heart shot or whatever one you choose. You certainly don't want to hit it in a spot that won't kill it cleanly.

This is where the professional stalker comes in: he knows how to go about getting a good position from which to shoot, he knows where and when to shoot the beast and so on.

But maybe the single most important thing about rifles – and guns too, for that matter – is safety. You must always, always, always open a gun when it is handed to you, to check that it is empty, that it is unloaded. If you are ever seen to pick up a gun and fail to check that it is unloaded, you should never be allowed to handle a firearm in the rest of your life. This is a very, very important thing, because a weapon can go off when you are least expecting it, sometimes for the most unlikely of reasons.

For instance, we got a gun back from the gun shop where it was in for repair, and it was supposed to have been fixed. But it hadn't been – and the moment you closed that gun, it went off. So that is why when you close a gun, you always turn away first from anybody standing in the vicinity. Obviously, it would not have been pointing at someone – anybody who ever points a firearm at anyone else, unloaded or not, should be jailed, in my opinion.

This safety aspect is the first thing you are ever taught when shooting, and if you can't get the hang of it then you aren't safe with a firearm and should never be allowed to handle one. And then it is up to you to see how good you can become – that's where the practice comes in, though some folk are natural shots and some aren't.

I got a lot of encouragement myself as a young lad, shooting clays and hares. The local farmer then had far more hares on his ground than he wanted, so that was great practice for me as a laddie.

I get my own guns from various places, sometimes used-gun shops, sometimes I just hear that so-and-so has a gun to sell, someone will phone up and say, 'Are you still looking for such and such a weapon?' And I'll buy it if the price is right. After

Geese in the long grass

all, if I buy a gun at, say, £300 and look after it, some day I might be able to sell it for £400. Naturally, the looking after is very important; you must clean a gun after every time you have used it, clean the barrel of gunpowder, oil all the moving bits, and have it overhauled at the end of every season by a proper gunsmith.

That way, you know they will work when you want them to work – and sometimes they will give you a shot that you don't forget in a hurry. I remember once a farmer came to me, he was having a terrible problem with foxes on his land, dead lambs all over the place. Nine nights I staked out that farm, and every night the fox was killing lambs and I just couldn't get him – he was always just out of range. so on the tenth I zeroed the rifle for three hundred yards – and that night I got him, broadside-on. I had been after him for a long time, every night, all night, and there he was, broadside-on. I just shot at him and he dropped stone-dead. He had killed something in the region of sixty lambs by the time I got him. But I got him – eventually, I did get him.

And another time, about three years later, I was coming along a track when I saw two foxes walking side by side, and obviously they hadn't seen me. Standing up, I could see two of them, but when I lay down to shoot I could only see one. Still, one dead fox is better than no dead fox. But when I had fired and walked up to the target, there were two dead foxes: the bullet had gone through the first and killed his mate just like that.

I suppose really I am very lucky compared to most people who are interested in guns because I get so much practice with all sorts of weapons, whether it be shotgun or rifle.

And being a keeper means that you are using firearms in a wide range of situations. With the rifle, it is the foxes and the deer; with the shotgun, it could be clays or pheasants or ground-game. Certainly, by the end of July you want to be pretty sharp with the shotgun – because in a week or so it's the Glorious Twelfth, the opening of the grouse season, and that's when the shotgun really comes into its own on the hills.

Troubled Tilt:
Somers in the Glen

O n Monday morning the 18 October, I set out on foot from Blair Atholl
Inn to visit the far-famed Glen Tilt. It was with some anxiety and
trepidation I entered that beautiful but precarious pass, guarded from public
intrusion by an impetuous duke and some score of stalwart hill-men.

I could not avoid reflecting on my solitary and defenceless condition, and
how easy it would be for the duke, in a fit of feudal rage, to immure me
in the dungeon of his castle, or bury me fathoms deep in some dark pool
of the Tilt.

I had been told at the village that the duke granted tickets of admission to
the glen when those were politely asked by respectable people; and one
obliging person even proposed to procure me one of these precious documents,
not much inferior in their magic powers to the Open Sesame of Ali Baba
and the Forty Thieves.

But I had also heard another story, which was to the effect that, from time
immemorial, the public had enjoyed right of way through the glen – that all
the old people in the parish, and many of the young ones, had exercised this
right oftener than they could count, and were prepared to swear that they
had seen with their own eyes the beaten track which they and their fathers
trod; and finally, that passengers were still in the practice, almost daily, of
making their way through the glen in equal contempt of ducal prohibition
and ducal leave.

Tickets from the Duke of Atholl, permitting access to Glen Tilt, are not
unlike the black-mail which Highland caterans levied upon Lowland cowards
for restoring the cattle which they had stolen from them – with this difference,

---

*The pomp and state in which this noble person
[the Duke of Atholl] lives, is not to be imitated
in Great Britain; for he is served like a prince, and
maintains a greater equipage and retinue than five
times his estate would support in another country.*

Daniel Defoe, *A Tour Through the Whole Island of
Great Britain*, 1724–6

125

that, in days when law and right are strong, it would be trebly disgraceful to yield to any such imposture. Accordingly I declined the obliging offer that was made to me, and mustering courage, resolved to try the fortunes of the day, unarmed with any other weapon than a just cause and a moderate-sized walking-staff.

The morning was grey and misty. It had rained heavily all night, and the fallen leaves that lay thick and soaked with wet upon the roads spoke in saddening terms of the rapidly declining year.

The time was ill-chosen for a good view of the glen; but as the object of my mission was not to admire its scenery, but to learn its history, its capabilities, and its present uses, this was a matter of less consequence.

At the entrance to the glen the hills recede on both sides and, flattening down their summits, round themselves into natural and easy union with the plain. As you scale the slopes, nothing can exceed the picturesque beauty of the view. The plain of Atholl lies stretched below you in the utmost magnificence – its numerous objects displaying themselves more minutely, and assuming a greater charm, the higher you ascend.

A few arable farms, of which the duke's home farm of Blair Walker is the principal, fill the mouth of the glen with rural plenty. The few houses on the opposite side seem so near that you may almost converse with their inmates; while down in the bottom of the glen, a profusion of wood covers the course of the Tilt, known at this point only by the noise of its waters among the rocks, and the thin line of spray which rises above the trees.

Ben-y-gloe and the higher mountains were capped with clouds, but there stood their mighty though veiled forms like landmarks, teaching the passenger of the glen what a long and devious route he has to tread. The road alternately dips into the shadows of deep woods and emerges into open glades; and at length guides you down to the bottom of the valley, where you must be content with a narrower prospect and less inspiring views.

The road is the most dangerous and the most horrible I ever travelled; a narrow path, so rugged that our horses were often obliged to cross their legs in order to pick a secure place for their feet; while, at a considerable and precipitous depth beneath, roared a black torrent, rolling through a bed of rock, solid in every part but where the Tilt had worn its ancient way.

Thomas Pennant, *Tour in Scotland,* 1771

Troubled Tilt: Somers in the Glen

> 🌿 *By feudal times there were forestry laws and the Royal Forests were preserved. The murder of the king's forester in Glenartney by some MacGregors in 1589 was the cause (or perhaps the excuse) for the intensification of the bitter persecution of their clan that ended in the proscription of its very name.*
>
> I. F. Grant, *Highland Folk Ways*

I took some delight in traversing the old roads and in tracing out the sites of the numerous dwelling-places with which the glen has at one time been thickly studded.

Formerly a seat of rural townships, Glen Tilt is now a scene of utter desolation.

The duke's lodge, two or three cottages inhabited by gamekeepers, and one empty and fast-decaying farmhouse, which is said to have sheltered under its roof seven of the crowned heads of Europe, are the only human residences remaining in a glen which must, at one time, have contained 400 or 500 people.

A gamekeeper or a gillie hurried past me occasionally, at the jog-trot peculiar to hill-men, as if dispatched on some mission of importance from the castle; and from them I learnt that the duke was expected to visit the lodge in the course of the day.

Not the slightest hint was given, however, that the glen was too small to contain both His Grace and me; and the few words about the shutting of the road that I was able to extract from the kilted guardians of the forest ran in the same humble and apologizing vein that I had remarked among the villagers of Old Blair.

Three hours' walking brought me to the duke's shooting-lodge, a plain building of one storey, situated lengthwise across the glen, and ornamented with evergreens, in the form of half a dozen square yards of Scotch kail. Here the new road ends, and the traveller to Braemar is conducted for the rest of his journey along what is known in the Highlands as a good bridle road. As I had no desire to penetrate the wilds of the Grampians, I began to retrace my steps to the plain of Atholl.

It is sufficient to say that I returned in the same unmolested way that I had gone, without receiving an uncivil word from anyone, and without encountering either hawk or chief.

A steady attempt has been making way for years to propagate the idea that the public have no right of access to the glen without the duke's

Troubled Tilt: Somers in the Glen

> *Whether the old forest is simply revived, or whether new regions are brought within that mystic circle for the first time, the same devastation preceded the completion of the enterprise. Houses, roads, enclosures, cattle, men – every work of time and of progress – are all extirpated by a word, in order that deer may enjoy the luxury of solitude, and sportsmen the pleasures of the chase.*
>
> Robert Somers, *Letters from the Highlands*

permission; and the stealthy progress of an opinion of this kind is more to be dreaded than those acts of violence into which the duke is occasionally betrayed.

The rebukes lately administered to His Grace will probably have the effect of putting him upon his guard; and, for the future, he may attempt, by an artful policy, what cannot be so easily accomplished by force. But it would be prudent to strike the iron while it is hot!

There can be little difficulty in establishing in a court of law the right of the public to free access to Glen Tilt. The old roads are there to speak for themselves. Many travellers, now in their graves, have left in works that have survived them glowing narratives of journeys which they have made along a beaten track from Braemar to Blair Atholl; and hundreds of living tourists could be found to bear similar and more recent testimony.

But above all, the tradition and practice of the people in the district would afford overwhelming evidence of the prescriptive right of way which the public have acquired through this convenient mountain-pass.

It is also to be borne in mind that, by the old Roman law of way, which is the foundation of the law in Scotland, it was declared that where the public had right of way over a man's property they were entitled, when the road was out of repair, to go over any part of his land they pleased.

The inconvenience that would accrue to tourists and men of science from the closing of Glen Tilt has been much descanted upon, and will be widely sympathized with; but the injury which such a despotic step would entail upon the people of the district would be infinitely greater.

It is in the clearance of the people from Glen Tilt that we must look for the foundation both of the attempt which has been made to destroy the public right of way through it, and of any difficulty there may be in placing that right beyond the reach of danger. Had Glen Tilt been suffered to retain its

128

population, any attempt to put it in a state of blockade would not only have been unsuccessful, but it would have been literally impossible.

So far as I can gather, the depopulation of Glen Tilt was effected between 1780 and 1790. This glen was occupied in the same way as other Highland valleys, each family possessing a piece of arable land, while the hill was held in common. The people enjoyed full liberty to fish in the Tilt, an excellent salmon river; and the pleasures and profits of the chase were nearly as free to them as to their chief.

But the present duke's grandfather acquired a taste for deer. The people were accustomed to take their cattle in the summer season to a higher glen that is watered by the Tarff; but a large dyke was built at the head of Glen Tilt, and they were forbidden to trespass, or suffer their stock to trespass, beyond it.

The outer region was consigned to the undisturbed possession of the deer. These light-hearted creatures increased in number, and paid no respect to their marches. They leapt over the enclosure, and destroyed the poor people's crops. The duke, observing this, gratified their roving propensities, and added a few thousand acres more to their grazing grounds at the expense of the people, who now began to be peeled of their possessions like one of their elms of its leaves by an October storm.

Gradually the forest ground was extended, and gradually the marks of cultivation were effaced, till the last man left the glen, and the last cottage

---

Sufferings have been inflicted in the Highlands scarcely less severe than those occasioned by the policy of the Norman kings. Deer have received extended ranges, while men have been hunted within a narrower and still narrower circle. One after one the liberties of the people have been cloven down. To kill a fish in the stream, or a wild beast upon the hills, is a transportable offence. Even to travel through the fenceless forest is a crime; and paths, which have linked hamlet with hamlet for ages past, have been shut and barred. These oppressions are daily on the increase; and if pushed much further it is obvious that the sufferings of the people will reach a pitch when action will be the plainest duty and the most sacred instinct.

Robert Somers, *Letters from the Highlands*

became a head of ruins. The same devastation which William the Conqueror, and the early Norman kings, spread over the plains of Hampshire, in the eleventh and twelfth centuries, was thus reproduced, at the end of the eighteenth, in this quiet Highland valley.

An event occurred at this period which afforded a pretext to the duke for this heartless extirpation of his people. Highland chiefs were exhibiting their patriotism by raising regiments to serve in the American war; and the Duke of Atholl could not be indifferent in such a cause. Great efforts were made to enlist the Glen Tilt people, who are still remembered in the district as a strong, athletic race. Perpetual possession of their lands, at the existing rents, were promised them if they would only raise a contingent equal to a man from each family.

Some consented, but the majority, with a praiseworthy resolution not to be dragged at the tail of a chief into a war of which they knew neither the beginning nor the end, refused. The duke flew into a rage; and press-gangs were sent up the glen to carry off the young men by force.

By impressment and violence the regiment was at length raised; and when peace was proclaimed, instead of restoring the soldiers to their friends and their homes, the duke, as if he had been a trafficker in slaves, was only prevented from selling them to the East India Company by the rising mutiny of the regiment!

He afterwards pretended great offence at the Glen Tilt people for their obstinacy in refusing to enlist, and – it may now be added – to be sold; and their conduct in this affair was given out as the reason why he cleared them from the glen – an excuse which, in the present day, may increase our admiration of the people, but can never palliate the heartlessness of his conduct.

His ireful policy has taken full effect. The romantic Glen Tilt, with its fertile holms and verdant steeps, is little better than a desert.

Adapted from Robert Somers, *Letters from the Highlands*

❧ AUGUST ❧

If there is one single day in the keeper's entire year that stands out above all others, it is of course the Glorious Twelfth – 12 August, and the first day of the grouse-shooting. For every gamekeeper who has grouse to look after, it is a day of the very first importance, and the start of a very busy time which could last for five or six months.

Although it is a busy day, it can also be a day of great pleasure, because it can demonstrate what the keeper has been doing for the previous few months in terms of looking after the grouse. So you always hope for a good day, and hope that the guns appreciate your efforts and the efforts of everyone else involved.

Every keeper should give the Glorious Twelfth the respect it deserves, and that means an early-morning start. All the work that can be done has been done, and it only remains to see what has come of it – so I suppose there is a bit of tension to the day as well.

The keeper starts off his day by appearing at the front of the lodge where he has arranged to rendezvous with his guests. He will have his tweed suit on, along with a shirt and tie, and will be looking very respectable. Probably all the under-keepers and other assistants will be there as well. It is a day when we all think about what we have done, think about what we are going to see shortly. And sometimes you can't help wondering about how keepers on other estates will get on as the day goes on, and about what sort of grouse-bags they will have had by the end of it.

It is always an exciting day to have your guests go to the hill, enjoy some good weather, eat well at lunchtime, and of course have a good day's sport. It is very, very important that every one of the guests enjoys themselves from start to finish, and that everything goes like clockwork.

Charlie and the lads from Forest Lodge with a party of guests before the start of the shoot on the Glorious Twelfth

There are two methods, mainly, of grouse-shooting on the moor. The first is the walk-up, where the entire party walks in line abreast, twenty to thirty metres apart, in extended line of guns, keepers and dogs. And then, when the grouse rise in flight from the ground before you, that's when you open fire. It takes a very experienced person to pick out the correct grouse, though an experienced shot can generally pick out an old cock for the first two weeks of the season.

The second method of grouse-shooting on the moor is driven grouse. That is when the guns are in a line of butts on the moor. Basically, they are simple open-topped hides, built usually of stone or wood or whatever – just something to hide the guns from the grouse, which fly overhead after being driven down on the butts by a line of beaters, who could be a mile or two away.

This takes a lot of skill. The keeper has to know his ground, know the effect of the wind on the birds, and know how they will fly in various wind directions. On days of high winds, the guns can be ready in the butts and the birds can take off in a completely different direction. But if everything goes as it should, then it can be very exciting for someone who is keen on shooting, because the grouse travel very quickly overhead.

I like shooting driven grouse myself. It is very skilled work to do properly, and it is perfect when you see the grouse driven down towards you in the correct manner. In my lifetime I have not had many days of shooting at driven grouse because generally it is very expensive, and it isn't the keeper's job to be shooting at them – it is the keeper's job to produce the grouse on the appointed day and make sure that the guests enjoy their sport. They are paying for it, after all, and sometimes quite a lot of money, because driven grouse-shooting is one of the most expensive shooting sports in Britain today. But it is a great experience for a skilled shot, there's no question about that.

If you are keen on shooting, and I have always been keen on it, driven grouse is super fun – pretty near as good as high-flying pheasant- and duck-shooting. In past days we also did a lot of hare-shooting, of course, and that takes a lot of skill too. When I was a young lad I used to keep count of the number of hares I had shot, and I was up around the thousand-mark, I think. In those days shooting hares was always done by the keepers in winter and early spring. But now, because of the way estate economies are, you can have foreigners shooting the hares. It can be fun to watch them, because some of them can get pretty excited.

In fact, they can be dangerous. It would be wrong to say that every one of them is dangerous, but certainly they are not as safe as British shots. Here, you are brought up with the importance of safety at the very front of your mind, but unfortunately some continentals – not all of them, only some – just don't seem to worry. I have seen one very bad accident in a grouse butt with a lady being severely shot. Fortunately, she didn't die, but accidents like that can certainly happen if everyone is not extremely careful every moment of the day.

Talking of foreigners, by the way, here's a favourite wee story about one of them. It was a friend of mine, a stalker, who was

A stop for refreshment

*Walk-up on the grouse moor: when the birds rise in
flight the party opens fire*

taking out a German for a stag. Well, they found one in due course, and the German was mad to have a shot. Now these Germans have excellent equipment, top-class rifles and superb 'scopes, and they don't miss very often at all. They do miss, but I would say very, very seldom. Anyway, this one was agitating to fire, but the beast was lying down and the stalker didn't think it was wise to shoot with it like that. Now the German didn't have as good English as most Germans do – and the stalker had a very broad Scots accent. The German was desperate to shoot, but my friend kept saying, in his broad accent, like, 'Not yet, not yet, he is leein' doon still'. But the German kept agitating and the stalker snarled at him, 'He's leein', ye fool, he's leein'! Jist wait till he gets on his feet'.

So in time the stag got up, and the German brought him down, and off they went for home. And the next day one of the other Germans came up to my friend and said, dead serious, 'Yesterday, you told my friend there was a lion on the estate. I will give you £100 if you let me shoot it.' I just wish I was there that day to hear my pal's explanation – just to hear it must have been wonderfully funny.

Anyway, that was just a wee story that sticks in my mind. I also like a lot of the traditions connected with the grouse-moor. I think it is terrific, after a morning's sport, to see a pony with panniers appear on the skyline in the distance and begin to make its way towards you. You know, it's the middle of the day, everyone is ready for lunch, and some of the lads are looking forward to a can of beer or a dram. It's great to see the pony and pony-man come over the brow of the hill – maybe he is still half an hour away, but you know he is coming straight for the butts.

It almost brings a tear to your eye when you think that in maybe ten or fifteen years there will be no more of this type of thing. Already there are fewer and fewer of them, and in future it will all be quad bikes and the like. That's what is happening: on the one hand a motorized thing with four wheels, and on the other something with four legs and four hooves, and I know which I prefer to see.

And there is also a lot of tradition connected with the way the grouse are prepared on the hill for collection. You lay out the birds in a very old-fashioned and traditional way. After all, they had

*Charlie explaining to guests how
to tell the age of a bird*

their last flight just an hour or two ago and, if they had survived it, they would have landed into the wind. So when you lay them out, you have their heads facing into the wind – facing the way they would take off and land.

You might wonder why we do it, but that is the way it has always been done. I have always been told in the past by keepers that that's the way to do the job – a wee bit of respect for the birds at the end of their lives.

And I would say the same sort of thing as far as one of their cousins goes too. He stays high up in the hills, usually above two thousand feet, and he is called the ptarmigan. He is a beautiful little bird with a fantastic camouflage in summer – and in winter, too, when he turns pure white. In the summertime he is a bluey-grey colour with tufts of white which represent the lichens and mosses on the high ground.

Grouse hanging in the larder at the end of a day's shoot

AUGUST

Now, you can be standing fifteen or twenty yards from a whole family of ptarmigan and the untrained eye would never so much as spot them. It's hard enough for the trained eye to see them, in fact. They will sit dead still, and it is not until they actually move that you see something that looks like the ground itself is moving and then you know what it is. You would think it was boulders moving in a field, or something like that.

In days past you could expect to find coveys of maybe a dozen or more birds. But, sadly, in the last few years we have not been so fortunate, and if we spot a covey of maybe six or seven birds we would consider ourselves as very lucky.

When I go out with a party shooting ptarmigan these days, I always remember a thing that happened to me perhaps twenty years ago with one of the old bosses I had. It was an invitation I had from one of the landowners right the way up in the top of Scotland. He was a great chap and a gentleman on the hill. He just loved his sport. He was a great shot too. He had spent many years in India, and the tales he could tell you about shooting snipe and duck there would make you think it was the finest place in the whole wide world.

In fact, he was a bit of a crackshot with a pistol as well. He once told me he had been a tea-planter, and in the evenings himself and his wife would sit on the veranda of their bungalow and have a drink. Now, in those days the done thing was to drink gin and tonic through the day because the weather was very hot and the gin kept you cool. But in the evening, when things had got cooler, you drank whisky.

There were cobras around the house. They would slither up towards the veranda, and he used to shoot them with a revolver before they got any closer. Now I quite believe the story to be true, because his wife did say once that she could remember him doing it. So you can imagine the two of them sitting there having a dram and all of a sudden there is this big snake right up on the veranda itself, and wriggling straight towards them – so he took up his .45 and just blasted the head off the thing.

Anyway, we had a fairly good walk that day, maybe a mile and a half, and this man was walking maybe twenty yards away from me, on very rough and rocky ground. I just happened to look round, and suddenly I saw him fall. He fell face-down and his gun went off, both barrels – I got a terrible fright. When I approached him he was still face-down, he hadn't moved an inch, and for the life of me I was sure that he was dead.

Anyway, thinking the very worst, I bent down and turned him over – and there he was, as large as life and with a big grin on his face. He was entitled to it, that's for sure. The only damage the gun had done was to have torn off the lapel on the left side of his shooting-jacket – it was shot clean off. Now both shots must have missed his throat by no more than an inch or two. He was a very lucky man that day.

The only thing he was really worried about was that he had broken the stock of his gun, and that was all he complained about. It was a very short-barrelled twelve-bore, maybe with a twenty-five-inch barrel or something like that, and it was his pride and joy. When we went back that night, the gun was in about four bits, the barrels all dented – and it wasn't the sort of gun that can be replaced or mended too easily either.

I can still remember him well. He spent the last years of his life in Scotland, and we loved going out together for maybe just two or three ducks: a wee afternoon's shooting and that was him content. Big bags he wasn't worried about, because he had seen more than enough of that in days gone by.

Aye, days do go by whether any of us like it or not. He said to me one morning that we were going to the hill to have a shot at some black game and so we fell in with them a bit later. Well, after a while we had ten birds bagged.

And then my friend dropped two birds with a brilliant right and a left – that's one shot from the right barrel and a second shot from the left barrel. He dropped the two birds stone-dead behind him, and out of the blue handed me his gun just like that. He said, 'Well, that's that, that's me finished with shooting.' Just like that, without warning. A brilliant right and a left – and his shooting days were over. The two of us were very nearly in tears to think that that was the way it was.

When we got home that day we had six brace. Not too bad really. But, all things considered, a sad sort of day too.

Tools of the Trade

The sporting rifle is not and never has been, despite the plausible portrayals of television and cinema screens, a weapon that charmingly combines sophistication of design and simplicity of use in one compact piece. It is not a precision instrument that the user just points – and the intended target obligingly falls down dead.

Certainly, the modern-day rifle is all of these things compared to its not-so-distant forebears. But to be used quickly and accurately under the difficult conditions of a deer-forest, it needs to be in the hands of an expert.

But expert as many professional hill-men are with the modern rifle, even they would have found the weapons of earlier times – and especially the first sporting guns – impossible to handle.

For the weapons of today offer everything that early weapons conspicuously did not: that is to say, long range, top hitting power, flat trajectory, high muzzle velocity, light weight, rapidity of fire, accurately machined barrels and breeches, ease and speed of operation, repeater and automatic firing, easy loading and reliable, simple-to-use ammunition.

Compared to the modern rifle, in fact, the primitive harquebus, prohibited in the time of Mary Queen of Scots, was a travesty of a firearm, as were its successor guns for at least three centuries. Their development was restrained on the one hand by the natural pace of technical development in engineering design, and on the other by an astoundingly conservative military establishment.

Indeed, so inefficient were firearms that, for centuries after the invention of gunpowder, the bow still outranged the musket; it was much more accurate, and had a much faster rate of fire – and it still had enough power to penetrate the armour of men and horses.

And, certainly, the bow and arrow – or just about any other manually powered weapon – was better suited to deer-hunting than the early gun. The matchlock appeared around the middle of the fifteenth century, but it was scarcely suited to efficient deployment in a deer-forest (it could not be used in or after rain, for instance).

A monster in terms of weight and calibre, its unrifled, smooth-bore barrel and ill-fitting ball of lead shot offered low muzzle velocity and a trajectory which meant that it was largely inaccurate at short ranges and entirely inaccurate at anything longer.

For a poacher, its flash, cloud of smoke and the stupendous noise it made when fired rendered it useless, and it was little better for any legitimate huntsman. Should he see a deer, and then get close enough to it, he could only hope that it would stay where it was long enough for the musket to be loaded and fired. Loading itself demanded an infinity of time relative to modern weaponry: first the charge would be measured out from the powder flask, wrapped, dropped down the muzzle and driven into place with the ramrod. Then the shot would be similarly treated. It did not help that these operations had to be conducted standing upright, either.

Next, the huntsman would measure some powder into the small priming tray at the side of the breech; with a flint and tinder he would strike into life the slow match to which the trigger was connected; aim at the target; and, finally, fire the weapon. This could be done only a few times (should there still be a stag or hind in the vicinity) before the weapon fouled up with unburnt powder, and no more shot could be rammed – or, in the case of some versions, hammered with a mallet – down the barrel.

Huntsmen as a consequence spurned the gun in favour of the long-established forms of coursing and driving with hounds; and military men of noble birth and senior rank scorned it as deeply unsporting.

(Noble or not, they did not overlook the cause of self-interest. For the development of the gun meant that any cowardly weakling, any lowly commoner, could knock an armoured knight off his horse, or the horse from under the knight, before gentleman or steed could commence that sporting slaughter of mere foot-soldier so long sanctified by custom, privilege and honour. This, in short, was sport no longer! Indeed, one sixteenth-century French commander ordered that any enemy soldier captured with a firearm should be done to death at once for breaking the rules of war; while a contemporary French author condemned the 'atrocity' of firearms on the field of war and boasted that France had never stooped to use these 'terrible weapons' against its enemies.)

Still, the musket survived the rebukes, and indeed appears to have been nourished by them, for over the next two centuries (in the course of which the French firearms industry made astonishing progress) its dominance as a weapon of war continued to grow, whether improved as wheel lock or further improved as flintlock.

It was simply a weapon whose time had come, at least on the field of battle – wondrously inaccurate and slow in operation as it was. It was, for instance, woefully off-target at anything over a hundred yards (and to hit anything under that required a musketeer of sniper standard). Indeed, it was commonly accepted that to kill a man required his weight in lead to be fired at him. And in battle, a musketeer would be lucky to get in one shot in an hour – and that only when the weather was dry.

But it was the weapon that (ignoring the unfortunate upset of the American War of Independence) extended and defended the British Empire in the eighteenth century; put 'Boney' Napoleon in his place; and with which Britain's regiments were happy to be armed almost until the time of the Crimean War.

It had served the military well, and they were for long disinclined to change to anything else, even when it was available to them.

And to the sportsmen, meanwhile, nothing was available other than their trusty muzzle-loaders, as Scrope and the Stuarts indicate only too well.

According to the former, who did all his stalking in the Forest of Atholl and who was clearly a very fine shot with his flintlock musket, *'It is seldom that you fire at a less distance than a hundred yards, and this is as near as I would wish to get. The usual range will be between this and two hundred yards, beyond which, as a general rule, I never think it prudent to fire, lest I should hit the wrong animal – though deer may be killed at a much greater distance.'*

Two problems associated with the muzzle-loader of the times were, first, the introduction of an incorrect amount of gunpowder, and, secondly, multiple-loading by mistake, in the heat of the moment – remarkably easy to do, as misfires were common.

> *The use of firearms for sport and hunting came some time after they were established as military weapons. The reason is not hard to understand. Early firearms were exceedingly clumsy and heavy; they were quite unsuited to being carried through forests. Further, the matchlock was almost impossible for hunting, not only because the mechanism was clumsy but because the light would almost certainly give away the position of the hunter unless he was exceptionally well concealed.*
>
> A. M. Low, *Musket to Machine Gun*

Scrope counselled:

> *Take care that the ramrods to your rifles be large and strong;*
> *they will otherwise be broken in the hurry of loading. I recommend*
> *you, moreover, to make one of your hill-men carry a very long*
> *and stout one in his hand, having a mark made in it at the length*
> *of your barrel, that you may ascertain the exact load. I used no*
> *other when this was at hand.*

The Stuarts, too, offered sound advice on the handling of these slow-loading weapons: *'In all kinds of deer-hunting, quick loading is no less important than a command of weapons, from the many unexpected changes which occur, and which are as often lost when a tardy hand has half loaded or is flurried with eagerness or haste.'*

The Stuarts, in common with all users of the flintlock, always wrapped the ball in a patch of material, to serve as a seal between the ill-fitting ball and the barrel (for any space between them meant leakage of the explosive force of the charge).

> *For the rifle, the tied balls are covered in kid leather patches,*
> *slightly dampened, and which, drying upon the balls, become*
> *fitted to them like moulds, when they are to be greased as usual.*
> *The tie is made very close and small, with silk thread, to which*
> *the superfluous leather is cut close, and the whipping, having*
> *only a few rounds, bursts, and loses the patch in the discharge.*
> *Balls thus prepared load with extraordinary ease and quickness,*
> *and, exploding the old barbarism of the hammer, are rammed down*
> *with a single push with the smoothness of a piston.*

But the Stuarts were writing in 1848 (Scrope was nine years earlier) and change could not be delayed indefinitely. Indeed, between 1850 and

---

I once found a huge brass .500 cartridge-case at the base of a small hummock where we were lying with our modern Holland and Holland .244 rifle. This old case dated back to 1900 or so, when black-powder Express rifles were in use. 'When they were fired a cloud of smoke surrounded rifle and stalker for moments afterwards': thus an old friend who had been a gillie in those days.

Lea MacNally, *Highland Year*

1900 there were as many changes in the military and sporting gun as there had been in the preceding five hundred years.

Principally, there were four interdependent breakthroughs, and they revolutionized the gun on both battlefield and deer-forest.

First came rifling – the spiral grooving inside the barrel, which gave spin to the bullet, leading to higher muzzle velocity, smaller calibres and flatter trajectories – which in turn offered much-improved potential accuracy.

Secondly, the long-established method of muzzle-loading gave way to breech-loading: faster in itself, and opening the way to multiple-shot weapons armed with a magazine in the stock, under the barrel or directly under the breech.

Thirdly, ammunition increasingly came in the form of a one-piece charge-and-bullet combination, slipped into the breech and quickly fired.

And, fourthly, the method of exploding the charge was radically changed. Instead of flint igniting a small pan of firing-power which, through a small hole in the side of the barrel, exploded the gunpowder charge, a detonating cap was fixed in the bottom of each of the new-fangled bullets. A firing-pin attached to the trigger then hit the cap, which in turn exploded the charge.

The day of the true rifle had at last arrived (though the bullet was still propelled by gunpowder), and one of its greatest exponents was Walter Winans, an eccentric American millionaire who was so keen on stalking that he even devised means of painting a good, but white, mare (with dye from a West End hairdresser) in the cause of camouflage. (It worked, too: when the mare was let loose in the paddock, the other horses, having failed to recognize her, kicked and otherwise attacked her.)

Winans, a brilliant shot who could easily fell a running stag at two hundred yards, was critical of the old style of large-bore guns, with a half-inch calibre and using four and a half drachms of black powder: *'Their weak points were the difficulty of judging distance from a hundred to two hundred yards, and the great noise of the explosion which made one shot frighten away most of the deer on a beat. The recoil'* – as may be imagined – *'also was very severe.'*

For Winans, 'The ideal rifle for deer-stalking would be one which shoots from ten up to three hundred yards without needing any alteration of elevation, giving a killing blow if the deer is struck anywhere near a vital place, makes no noise, and is light to carry; incidentally, also having very small, light cartridges, and loading automatically and noiselessly.'

Winans, who for some years re-introduced the old form of deer-driving to his 200 000-acre stalking-ground in Ross-shire, favoured double-barrelled rifles (they offered better balance than a single-barrelled weapon), firing bullets that did a minimum amount of damage to a deer – unlike the lead ball of the older type of gun.

On his Express rifle, he favoured the use of a sling, and was particular about its paint-scheme: dull grey to prevent glint, apart from the fore sight, which would be over-large and matt white.

> *The great thing for deer-stalking is to have a front sight which enables one to obtain an approximately true alignment instantaneously, rather than one for extremely accurate aim when time is no object and the light is perfect. Most deer are shot in a bad light, early in the morning or late in the afternoon, so that too fine sights are a mistake.*

So successful was the Express rifle – introduced in the 1850s – that it swept away the older style of gun in a matter of years – and, with it, an older style of deer-hunting.

By 1892 deerhounds had gone for ever from the hills, as the evidence of one survey discloses. Glenartney, Comrie: *'The explosive bullets have finished the dog's work. No dogs of any kind are used here.'* Invercauld: *'The seldomer dogs are used in the forest the better. In my opinion the Express rifle has done for the dogs.'* Applecross: *'No dogs used here in deer-stalking. In former years, eight were used. The Express rifle has done away with deerhounds in forests.'* And from Blackmount: *'About thirty years ago there were as many as sixty deerhounds kept here. Deerhounds were entirely given up five years ago. Since the introduction of breech-loading rifles and explosive bullets, the help of a dog is seldom required in shooting deer.'*

And two final improvements were shortly to be added. The first, common nowadays on stalking-rifles, was the telescopic sight. Actually, these had been used as far back as the Indian Mutiny of 1856 (which had in part been started by the rumour that the patches for flintlock balls were to be greased with pig and cow fat – offensive and sacred to Muslim and Hindu respectively). The First World War saw urgent development in this field, but for many years such weapons were considered unsporting in the deer-forest.

The second was much more important, and made possible by newly discovered chemicals like cordite, which were smokeless and more powerful – once again the performance of the rifle was hugely improved.

The introduction of these new forms of 'gunpowder' meant less noise and less smoke from the weapon. Improved velocity meant a flatter trajectory and greater accuracy. More power meant smaller calibres, which meant lighter weapons and lighter ammunition – which meant the stalker could carry more of it.

Tools of the Trade

*I like, if possible, to shoot at running deer
the moment they are landing over a burn. By
watching where the leading hinds land in jumping a
burn or other obstacle in their course, you can often
get a stag as he follows at the same place. If a
stag stops, the rest often hesitate and give you
a good chance.*

Walter Winans, *The Sporting Rifle*

Massive weapons were still available. In 1903 the gun-making firm of Jeffery introduced their double 600-bore rifle and smokeless cartridge. Regulated for a charge of 120 grains of cordite and a 900-grain bullet, it had a muzzle energy of 8700 feet-pounds. In 1910 it cost, with doll's-head extension, £65.

But for the deer-forest such rifles were simply far more powerful than any stalker required. The day – and it was a long one – of the .303 had arrived. At the turn of the century Lady Breadalbane, a notable shot, acquired for herself one of these newfangled toys and reported it 'unsurpassed' for lightness and quickness in handling; it was also relatively silent, with *'no recoil and no concussion to give headaches'*.

Shortly, just about every keen deer-stalker would be converted to the .303. And it was a rifle that would serve stalkers (legitimate and covert) until very recently, with the introduction of even smaller-calibre rifles like the near-ubiquitous .270 and .243 of today.

What will replace them remains to be seen. But the sporting rifle has always followed developments in the military rifle – and the next generation of military rifles (indeed, some already in use) offer advanced night-sights for poor-visibility shooting and even laser-sights. The rifle of the future may be silent: it may fire a lethal laser-beam or a sonic 'bullet' that kills, disables or merely stuns the target.

Or – in an age that finds the slaughter of animals for sport increasingly outrageous – the day may yet arrive of the sporting paint-rifle, doubtless to be had with silver-engraved breech and carved walnut stock.

But, as ever, it will be the man or woman in whose hands it is held that will make of it the weapon it is.

❧ SEPTEMBER ❧

Well now, September. That's us on the run-in to the back end of the year and of course what you could maybe call the main part of the year: the deer-stalking, taking parties out after the stags. In a good few ways you could say that it is even more important than the grouse – and certainly you get a different kind of party coming for the stags.

They are usually more individual. Rather than a large party, you get a group of perhaps three or four friends. But overall you could say they are a bit less gregarious than the folk who come up for the grouse. It's a different sort of sport, of course, a different sort of shooting – and I don't suppose it is any surprise that you get a different sort of personality attracted to it.

Obviously, a rifle isn't a shotgun: they are both deadly weapons, but a rifle has the range – and you have to be extremely careful about how you use it. We have to make sure that these people are capable of hitting the stags we stalk for them. Remember, they're shooting up to about a distance of, say, 200 yards, but a bullet can easily travel a mile or more and still be lethal. So they must be capable of hitting a target at least 150 yards away, with a five-inch bull, and hitting that bull three or four times out of five. A quick bit of practice makes all the difference, because as a rule these people are pretty good shots anyway – but, like anyone else, like anything else, they get rusty if they don't keep their hand in.

Probably, some of them haven't done any shooting for a long time. One thing's for sure, and that's that they won't have been doing much shooting in London if that's where they have come from.

So when they come up here we encourage them to do as much practice as possible before they actually go stalking. And of course we encourage them to use a good rifle of a proper calibre, along with a decent telescopic sight – that is very important.

Of course, most of the people we see have been at the job for a very long time and know the ropes inside out. But now and again there are first-timers, and I take great delight in introducing them to their first stag. I mean, I remember mine – it's something you never forget – and I hope that they will always remember their one. It is their holiday, it is their bit of fun. After all, they are often mad keen on the hill, but it doesn't matter how wealthy they might be, they can still only afford to get up there for two or three weeks in the year. At times, you know, I feel sorry for them, having to spend most of their time living and working in places like London.

So we go out of our way to make sure that they have the best sport available, to show them which stag we want shot, and to make sure that they place the bullet in the right place for a clean kill every time. That is their job. It is our job to get them close enough to the right stag, whether it is on its own or in the middle of a 200-strong herd. Sometimes it's a young beast that isn't going to improve, or an old one past his best; or it might even be what we call a trophy head.

Charlie following deer from the Land-Rover

*Stalking in
the glen*

That's a beast with the sort of antlers that people want to take home with them and stick on the wall. The antlers fall off in the spring and start regrowing immediately. They are covered with a soft tissue that we call velvet. Come August they are grown, although they have long strips of velvet hanging from them. It falls off in time, or the stags rub it off on whatever they can use. You can quite often pick up the strips of velvet on the hill and a lot of people say, 'What is that?' It looks like velvet, and that is exactly what it is. Sometimes people will even put some in their pocket as a sort of souvenir.

The best trophy heads are Royals, with six points on either side of the antlers: six even points on either side of his head, with the top ones so arranged that you should be able to sit a whisky glass in them. That's the real 'Monarch of the Glen' sort of trophy head that people want to see on their wall. When the hunter shoots his Royal he is a proud man, especially if he is a German – they are very keen on a good head to display when they get back home.

Of course, in the old days, when it was the gentry who tended to go after the stags, the stalker got the heads as part of his wages. But nowadays, because all these continental and foreign people want to have them on their walls back home, they don't stay with the stalker any more. Normally, the guest will say, 'I want that one to take away with me as a trophy', so that's when we have to prepare it for them.

We leave it hanging on the animal overnight, because in the morning the neck is stretched and that makes the job of skinning the beast easier. We cut the back end right through the top of the head, through the brain cavity, right down to the top of the back teeth, slip it off there with a very sharp, thin saw, and then you boil it. The bothy boys usually do this. They boil it up for maybe three-quarters of an hour and then skin off the rest of the meat.

Then we prepare the trophy, though the hunter often likes to do this himself – it is part of the ritual. But what I recommend is the way we do it ourselves – boil it in bleached water, which makes it pure white. Then you mount the antlers on a plaque, along with the name of the person who shot it, and where and when it was shot, before it gets hung in the gun-room or wherever you might want to put it.

Of course, there are sometimes stags with other sorts of antlers – what we call a 'switch'. A switch has a long spear-point coming out on either side of the head, a bit like two long, curved swords, and they are extremely sharp. Normally, when you get two stags fighting they have more or less the same type of antlers, which sort of bind together and all they can do is push at each other; they can't do much damage or harm to each other. But it's a different matter with the switch, with these long swords at either side of the head: they can go right through the normal set of antlers and stab the other beast.

This has happened many times. It's a great shame, but they often kill the other stag. Most of this sort of fighting takes place around the time of the rut, the breeding season. It starts around the twentieth of September, though sometimes it can be later than that, sometimes as much as two or three weeks later on one estate, but starting at the normal time on other estates. A wrong start to the rut isn't good news for the calves. It means they will be that bit younger come the spring, and of course that makes them a bit more vulnerable to bad weather and so on.

Now the actual rut is when the stag herds up groups of hinds – you could call it his private harem. You always know when the rut is about to start, because the stags begin to roar. The roaring is when the hormones in the body say that it is time to breed, and at times it is a sound you would hardly believe possible. But you don't forget it if some night up at Forest Lodge a stag comes towards you and he starts roaring – it makes the hair on the back of your neck creep!

He will try and cover most of these hinds in the time he can keep them to himself. Sometimes there might be fifty or even one hundred of them. He will go round and round herding them. When you look up the hill it is just like a collie dog herding sheep, but in actual fact it is the stag protecting his hinds and keeping them from escaping to another stag. He is always wary that another stag is going to appear and steal some of his hinds, and of course he has a good idea that if the other stag is about his size and weight then he will have a fight on his hands.

A lot of it is ritual – rocking back and forward for a while, and then they will run towards each other, their antlers will clash, and

LEFT *Preparing
to gralloch
a stag*

RIGHT *Charlie with
a guest beside
her kill*

BELOW *Dragging
the deer from
the hill*

they will start the fight. It is more of a pushing match than anything else, and whoever gets tired of it first is probably the loser. If the challenger gives up, then the first stag can go back to herding his hinds again. But of course he could face another challenger almost at once, and he still has to find time to cover the hinds – so it is a busy time for the stags, whether they are protecting their harem, or challenging to take one over.

This rut goes on for about three weeks, and at the end they are pretty exhausted. Of course, the better condition the stag is in at the beginning, the longer he can survive and cope. And it helps too if he gets in among the hinds before another stag does.

LEFT *Loading a stag onto the
pony with Paul's help*

BELOW *Loading a deer onto
the Land-Rover*

So these are the beasts that shooting parties are going after in September and October. They can be any sort of people, from maharajas to ordinary working people who spend most of their time in the bank or the post office or whatever. In the old days it was always the very well-off, but these days you can also get local people who save up their pennies for a couple of stags – although, if you really want value for money, you would be better at the hinds later in the year.

You might get three hinds in a day for the price of just one stag in the autumn. So that has been one big change in the last fifty years or so – in those days it was the millionaire sort who took a shooting-lodge, often for a whole season. If they liked it, and couldn't buy the forest, they could end up leasing it for years on end – quite a lot of people used to do that. But nowadays that sort of thing would be very expensive, and we are seeing people from a far wider range, in terms of both occupation and country of origin.

We see quite a few from South Africa and America – and of course from the Continent. Mind you, the end of the Iron Curtain has meant that hunting in Eastern Europe has been opened up in recent years, and there is some very good deer-stalking there – and not too expensive either. So that has sucked away some of our customers. But we still get people from what you might call the middle of the Continent – from Germany and Belgium and Denmark – as well as Americans and Canadians and quite a lot of British people, I am glad to say.

We find that British people understand a bit more about the way of life here, and about the way we conduct red-deer stalking. Of course, that is pretty natural – and we make big efforts to show the foreign guests how we do it here, because they have their own methods back home. Some of them are used to waiting in a seat half-way up a fir or an oak tree, just waiting for the deer to come out of the wood. That's because most of their shooting is done in heavily wooded areas. But in Scotland, even though we call them deer-forests, in actual fact the stalking is usually done on the open moor or rocky hill-ground.

I find that when foreigners come here and we show them the ropes, they find our way of stalking far more exciting – and that's why we sometimes get hunters from Africa, and professionals from Germany and Austria. I think they keep coming back because they like the way we do it here. And I am proud to say that it does seem to work – as long as the person has it in him or her to actually pull the trigger when the moment comes, and kill the stag.

A rifle must have an interest in the kill. They must have the metabolism to be able to say, 'I am capable of shooting to kill'. If you don't have that, bring your camera because that is the only thing you will be able to shoot with.

Even if you can do it, you must have the right gear for the hill, boots and waterproofs in particular. It can be nice in terms of

ABOVE *The dog handler with labradors at the grouse shoot*
OPPOSITE *Charlie leading off on the moor at the start of the shoot*
PRECEDING PAGE *Charlie taking a break during the grouse shoot*
OVERLEAF *The road from Glen Tilt to Carn a' Chlamain*

Roe deer on the hills

A guest with his first kill,
his face blooded

OVERLEAF *Frozen waterfall*
near Forest Lodge, Glen Tilt

weather well into September, but it can turn nasty as well. Camouflage clothes will do the job, but the best of the lot is a plusfour suit. They don't come cheap and they are not absolutely mandatory, but they are recommended. After all, they have been worn for a very long time, and there is usually a good reason for that. And then, of course, you will need a proper firearm and a certificate to use it.

So, you find an estate that will take you, and then you have to make sure you get to the place on time. You usually have to contact the stalker. Once you have done that he will give you all the do's and don'ts: advice about clothes, what sort of food to take to the hill and so on. Some people take a can of beer, some take a flask of coffee, some take a drop of whisky with them. It is entirely up to your own preference.

Myself, though, 1 prefer a good hot cup of tea or coffee on the hill with two or three good sandwiches – a dram is OK if you are on your way home. Indeed, it is even better when you get home. As everyone knows, or should know anyway, it can open the pores and let the cold in, and if you have to lie in a burn for three hours waiting for a stag to stand up and you have already half-emptied your whisky flask, then you are going to get really cold.

So, having found your stalker and arranged to meet him, arranged all your kit and so on, you follow the directions to the shooting-lodge where you are going to rendezvous.

Some people are a bit bemused when they first meet the stalker. They don't know that the wind plays a big part in where the deer are, and some of them really think you are a bit crazy when you walk out of the door in the morning and stand looking at the sky for five minutes. But you are looking very carefully to find out the direction of the wind, because basically that rules your day. You check the clouds, the trees, the smoke from any chimneys ... because wherever the wind is from, that decides where you are going to go in the next few hours.

For the guest, it is always important to be there bang on time. It looks good that you are interested, and if you are a wee bit early it is a wee bit more exciting for you. There is an element of excitement, especially for first-timers. Generally it starts the night before, though for some folk it starts a week or two before!

They are looking forward to it so much, especially if they have already got a taste for it – maybe after two or three kills, you have really been bitten by the bug and you want to carry on doing it for as long as you can. But for the first-timer – well, nobody really knows for certain what is going to happen.

The stalker will take you up and explain things to you, probably point out the area you will be stalking in, tell you that the deer are in such and such a place. He hands you a pair of binoculars and says, 'Look for them there', and all of a sudden, just out of the blue, you can see them on the hillside. You see all these tiny brown dots walking about, and you think, How on earth could I have failed to see all these deer earlier?

And then, having found them, you start the long stalk-in – and hope that by the end of the day it will have been a rewarding one for everyone concerned. You start the stalk, trying to keep track of where the deer are at all times as you move in, because they can smell you and see you at well over a mile – and if they do, they will move.

So it is very important to do what the stalker says, because you must stay out of sight and smell of the deer until you get into the position that you need to be in. This is the stalker's job – to get you to a spot from which you can bring down a stag. He will explain to you on the way what you have to do, whether crawling up a burn, or maybe down it, or whatever.

You can crawl through water, rocks, heather, moss, bogland – and at all times you must be behind the stalker until you are ready to come forward. Then you should be in a position from which you can actually shoot the stag. The stalker will tell you which one he has selected for you. Then he will slip the rifle out of its cover and hand it over. It is then up to you to shoot true.

You put the stock to your shoulder, lay your head against the stock, and look through the telescope until you find its cross-hair sights. Slowly, it goes up the side of the stag, creeps along to the heart position – and bang! It is the exciting part, that, when you squeeze the trigger with a loud crack of the weapon. The stag runs twenty, thirty, forty yards – and drops down dead.

If it is your first stag, the next stage is the blooding – you get the traditional blooding, just a wee drop of blood from the stag

SEPTEMBER

Drying out antlers at Forest Lodge

on the side of your face. Most people like to get their picture taken with their first kill, and then the gralloching starts, and finally the job of getting the beast home. Shooting the beast isn't the hard part of the job – but getting it home can be. The old traditional way was to carry it on your back with a rope over your shoulder, but ponies are obviously a much better way. Highland ponies are trained to do the job, and have specially designed and built saddles to help them.

The stag is loaded in a special way. Its head is doubled back on its body and usually tied down with leather straps. It takes two good strong lads to lift it up, because it can weigh fourteen, fifteen stone – sometimes even as much as twenty stones, or two and a half hundredweights. Once it is up, you have three straps to hold it in place: chest strap, neck strap and tail strap.

Then you can set off for home. The pony knows the way, of course, which is a lot more than you can say about the modern vehicles we use to take a beast off the hill. These days all-terrain vehicles, ATVs, are very popular for the job, and there is a good reason for it. With a pony you always needed two men, but with quad bikes and the like, one man is enough.

It's sad, but that's the way things are. Mind you, not much has changed for the stalker. We can be out all week on the hill, more or less every day on the hill, creeping through bogs and crawling up and down burns, right through September and on to the twenty-first of the following month, before we get a rest.

So, by the time that the stag-stalking closes, I can tell you, we are looking forward to a wee break. We're quite happy to leave the stags to themselves for another year!

Glen Tilt:
Poachers and Potentates

In the long history of deer-hunting in the Forest of Atholl, no single name is more illustrious than that of William Scrope, the Victorian enthusiast who spent ten years quartering Glen Tilt in enthusiastic pursuit of his quarry. Scrope, some of whose guns are still at Blair Castle, eventually knew the ground with an intimacy born of long familiarity.

As he describes it:

> The celebrated Forest of Atholl comprehends a vast tract of moor and mountain, about forty miles in length. It measures 135 451 acres. The part of the forest which is kept for deer-stalking is 51 708 acres, and is bounded chiefly on the west by Craig Urrard and the river Bruar; on the north by the Tarff; on the east by the Felaar grouse ground; and on the south by the cultivated grounds and woods of Blair. All this vast tract is reserved exclusively for deer, with a slight exception as to Glen Tilt, where sheep are occasionally permitted to pasture.
>
> In the year 1776 the number of deer in all the forest did not probably exceed 100; though some small herds have wandered in it from time immemorial. The great increase took place in the year above mentioned when Forest Lodge was built, the sheep and cattle removed, and the hills were thus free from disturbance. Favoured and protected as they now were, the increase became very rapid; so that of late years their numbers were computed at about seven thousand.

Of the forest, Scrope was apt to wax lyrical. He writes:

> The ground is in all respects the most favourable that can be imagined for a forest. Mountains of various altitude, open sunny corries, deep glens and ravines, holes for solitary harts to hide in, and numerous rolling pools, burns also and rivers, and large pine woods to shelter them during the inclement season.
>
> The two highest mountains in the forest are Ben-y-gloe and Ben Dairg or the Red Mountain. Ben-y-gloe is of vast magnitude, and comprehends a little territory within itself, stretching its huge limbs far and wide. It is computed to be twenty-four Scotch

miles in circumference, and it contains twenty-four corries; these
corries, though contiguous, are separated from each other by such
high ridges, that a person standing on one of them could not hear
a shot fired in the next.

But it was with the deer that Scrope, as so many before and after, was mainly concerned, and *The Art of Deer Stalking* is packed with descriptions of successful hunts.

Here, for instance, is just one, typical of the days of black-powder rifles and dogs, when we find Scrope on the hill with the celebrated gamekeeper, Peter Fraser.

Putting the rifles on the heather, they *'put their caps in their pocket and crept forward on their hands and knees to a large granite block; then, cautiously peering over its summit, they began to examine the ground with their telescopes steadily poised upon it'*. Having thus spied a stag, they reckon they can get within a hundred yards of it *'and that is near enough in all conscience'*.

The stalk then begins: four men, two hounds and a number of heavy rifles. The chosen stag is obscured by hinds, so the party works its way through a bog, then up the length of a burn, and back into the bog, always taking immense pains to ensure that they are never upwind of the beasts. At last, having crossed a particularly exposed piece of ground, Scrope worked his way, carrying the rifles, up a second burn, to his waist in water. The rest of the party then followed.

In breathless expectation they now turned to the eastward, and
crept forward through the bog, to enable them to come in upon
the flank of the hart, who was lying with his head upwind, and
would thus present his broadside to the rifle – and all this one
brief moment might render futile, either by means of a single
throb of the pulse in the act of firing, or a sudden rush of the

---

In 1770 the Atholl forester Paul Robertson reported finding four army officers shooting on the duke's best moor. When he confronted them, they asked if he had a warrant from the duke for preserving his hills. He told them he had. They then desired him to stop the warrant in his backside, and were very abusive to him.

Duff Hart-Davis, *Monarchs of the Glen*

Glen Tilt: Poachers and Potentates

> 🌼 *Burning the water was practised in the*
> *eighteenth century. The fish were attracted to the*
> *surface at night by means of a torch and were then*
> *speared with a leister, a pronged iron fork. Guddling*
> *trout with the hand as they lie under the bank or*
> *slipping a loop of fishing-line over the tail of a*
> *resting salmon, or spearing him with a gaff or pole*
> *needs no special equipment and are no doubt still*
> *carried on. I have seen wickerwork traps that were*
> *set in the narrow part of a burn.*
>
> I. F. Grant, *Highland Folk Ways*

deer, which would take him instantly out of sight. The tops of
his horns alone were to be seen, no more: a moment's pause,
when the sportsman held up his rifle steadily above the position
of the hart's body; then, making a slight ticking noise, up sprang
the deer; as instantly the shot was fired, and crack went the ball
right against his ribs.

But on this occasion Scrope had not brought the beast down and, badly wounded, it fled, pursued by the hounds. At length the hart turned at bay in a rocky burn at the foot of a waterfall, trapped there by the dogs until Scrope could come up. At close range he killed the beast with a single shot. A staunch round of whisky stiffened the gentlemen for the gralloch. A second round celebrated the conclusion of the matter, and the dead stag was marked with a pile of peat to assist later collection by estate pony.

Scrope was a product of a classical education at Eton and Oxford. Whether he was in the same league as some other, less official, stalkers in the Forest of Atholl is open to serious question. Among these can be counted the great poachers, Alexander Davidson and John Farquharson.

Davidson, born in the 1790s, was reckoned to be one of the handsomest men of his generation, and tremendously powerful. A superb dancer in the traditional style, he was also a man of extraordinary endurance. Beginning his life as a gamekeeper on land rented from the Duke of Atholl, he soon became more or less a full-time poacher, given to warning landlords that he would be traversing their land at such and such a time *en route* to another estate, and informing them that he would shoot nothing unless it crossed his direct line of travel.

167

> *There were two missionaries from a far-out sect
> in the village once, and they were forever at the
> house with their leaflets. Then one night we came home
> with a hind and gralloched it in the shed. Just as we
> were burying the guts in a hole at the back gate by the
> light of a Tilley lamp, the missionaries appeared out
> of the night. But they didn't hang around. And we
> never saw them again after that.*
>
> Anon

A superb shot and stalker, he roamed and hunted largely at will across three or four counties for three or four months a year. When he died in 1843, his successor John Farquharson was already busy on the hills.

Farquharson was another shot of genius. His family had lived in the area for generations, and Farquharson took the view – as did so many of his kind – that he had a considerably greater right to bird, beast or salmon than any holidaying and amateur sportsman, fresh-faced from London on the newfangled steam trains. The fact that poaching was prohibited, and this prohibition enforced, only made a greater sport of poaching. For if any fool could (and can) get a stag with the assistance of a party of retainers, it took (and takes) a cool hand, a good scout and an expert shot to take one under the noses of the keepers, stalkers, watchers and other retainers of 'the sporting interest'.

A one-time gamekeeper himself, Farquharson was a noted shot on the national scale, winning many prizes and responsible for a number of innovations in the field of marksmanship. He was convicted a number of times for poaching, the savagery of the fines suggestive of the extent to which the courts victimized the lone shot. In 1884, for instance, he was fined £25 for poaching some grouse that he had had sold in London at their absolute peak price on 12 August for just less than £14.

And two years later he was fined £33 with the option of eighty-eight days in jail. What he thought of this has not been recorded, but in his fearless and inveterate hunting may be guessed great eloquence. He died, in spirit unbeaten, in his own bed in 1893.

But Davidson and Farquharson – amid who knows how many others, before and since – went out of their way to keep their hunting discreet. Others – if not exactly in the same league as shots – had no need for such discretion.

Not least of these were Queen Victoria and her husband, Prince Albert.

Glen Tilt: Poachers and Potentates

They had first visited the Highlands in 1842. Two years later they were back, on this occasion as guests at Blair Castle, along with a large retinue including Charlotte Canning, a lady-in-waiting to the twenty-five-year-old queen. The standards they set are not likely to endear themselves to the modern shot, however.

Lady Canning reported:

> *The Prince was to shoot a fat stag from the window. A few of these were caught when young and put in a sort of park - the others came to them and there is a spot they jump down and cannot get back from and the park now has a very good herd in it. The rifle was brought into the dining-room and the fat stag chosen. The queen went to a window of another room and looked out. I saw the poor beast catch up his legs for an instant and then look round surprised and walk a few steps and then die – they say it was well shot through the heart. The other stags walked quietly away and the dead hart was brought round to the door on a horse for the queen to look at him. It was quite a Landseer picture, all the tents and the Highlanders on guard for a background and the dead deer and the pony standing by him, a number of picturesque kilted keepers. . . .*

At this event Victoria shook and was 'very uncomfortable', though the discomfort did not dissuade her from watching a similar performance the next day – having sent for Lady Canning by way of support.

But the ladies quickly graduated to the sterner climes of Glen Tilt, and, while Albert did the shooting, his adoring wife sketched and watched the action of an old-style deer-drive from a suitable viewpoint.

Landseer, who painted the Monarch of the Glen, *laid claim to a number of other artistic talents. He spent many Victorian autumns shooting and sketching with the second wife of the sixth duke of Bedford on the duke's Highland deer-estate. But, though young enough to have been her son, it is now accepted that he fathered at least two of her ten children. As Sir Walter Scott observed, without apparent irony, the duke acquired the estate 'to gratify the duchess's passion for the heather'.*

Duff Hart-Davis, *Monarchs of the Glen*

Glen Tilt: Poachers and Potentates

As Victoria herself recorded:

> *We sat down on the ground, Lady Canning and I sketching, and Sandy and Mr Oswald lying on the grass and looking through glasses. After waiting again some time, we were told in a mysterious whisper that 'they were coming', and indeed a great herd did appear on the brow of the hill, and came running down a good way when most provokingly two men who were walking on the road – which they had no business to have done – suddenly came in sight, and then the herd all ran back again and the sport was spoilt. My poor Albert had not even fired one shot for fear of spoiling the whole thing, but had been running about a good deal.*

On a later occasion the royal party proceeded up Glen Tilt in carriages, for a classic stalking-outing of the time. Albert and the queen walked about a bit, as Victoria recorded in her journal,

> *and then Lady Canning and we mounted our ponies and set off on our journey, Lord Glenlyon leading my pony the whole way, Peter Fraser, the head keeper (a wonderfully active man) leading the way; Sandy and six other Highlanders carrying rifles and leading dogs, and the rear brought up by two ponies with our luncheon-box. Lawley, Albert's Jaeger [rifleman], was also there carrying one of Albert's rifles; the other Albert slung over his right shoulder to relieve Lawley. So we set off and wound round and round the hill, which had the most picturesque effect imaginable. As we ascended we had to speak in a whisper, as indeed we did almost all day, for fear of coming upon deer unawares. The wind was, however, right, which is everything here for the deer. I wish we could have had Landseer with us to sketch our party, with the background.*

On this occasion Albert missed the only shot of the day, but he was to improve somewhat. On the last day of their Highland holiday, Victoria was again out on the slopes of Glen Tilt in her role of deer-drive spectator. And Lady Canning later wrote:

> *I was told of an immense herd and saw at a distance a hill that looked as if covered with brown fern, but the brown hill-side seemed to move, and the herd came on for nearly two miles. The hill-side was alive with them and we could hear their bellowing and the sound of their feet, with a glass we could see them beautifully. From our bird's-eye view we could see both prince*

Glen Tilt: Poachers and Potentates

> *The twentieth-century poacher is an ill-conditioned, lazy, drunken and slinking scoundrel, an enemy to law and order, without a particle of true sportsmanlike feeling in his veins. Taken as a class, poachers are a set of hardened criminals, careless of everything but their own besotted lives – a grain in the sediment of society. Drink has him, as a rule, in its grip. He has a shifty and congested eye, and a tremulous tongue. He is a friend of no man and an enemy to most, and is in the majority of cases an arrant coward.*
>
> A. S. Walker and P. J. Mackie, *The Keeper's Book*

and deer at once when they could not see each other and it was interesting beyond anything to watch their stalking – how near he got sometimes without knowing it.

In this herd there were around 2000 beasts, but at the last moment they panicked and ran and the prince missed all of five shots (though it is unlikely that any was an easy one). Consolation came later that day, however, when Albert killed *'a fine hart in the wood just before dark'*.

The next day Albert and Victoria headed again for London, where the Foreign Secretary among others was soon to hear of the wondrous Highlands and their picturesque natives. *'Lord Aberdeen'*, she wrote, *'was quite touched when I told him I was so much attached to the dear, dear Highlands and missed the fine hills so much. There is a great peculiarity about the Highlands and the Highlanders; and they are such a chivalrous, fine, active people. Our stay among them was so delightful.'*

The royal couple were back in the 'dear, dear Highlands' in 1847, and although the rain was gracelessly relentless, it did not dissuade them. A year later they took a lease on a little castle near Braemar, called Balmoral.

And the cult of the nineteenth-century deer-forest was under way with a vengeance.

171

❧ OCTOBER ❧

By now nobody is in any doubt that the summer is past. By this stage we are well into the autumn and thinking about the coming winter. Of course, you can get a good autumn well into October and maybe even beyond, but you can get some really nasty ones as well!

Not that it makes much of a difference anyway, because whatever the weather might be throwing at us there is always the sheep to attend to, as well as stalking for the hinds.

When we are hind-shooting we usually have a few guests, people who can't really go after the stags for one reason or another. Maybe people whose work is too important, so that they can't get away to the hill at the proper time of year for the stags, but are still keen on field sports.

Sometimes it is simply a matter of cost. It is slightly cheaper to shoot hinds in October, and even earlier in September. Obviously, they can't get all of September because the stags are on the go and we are at them every day, but by October there are plenty of opportunities to have a go at the hinds.

We have to accommodate just about anyone for the hind-shooting because it is money for the estate. But we don't personally like to take on a great number of guests for the hinds, because we have so many of them to cull and we just like to get on with the job. In the autumn the weather can start to play up and get in the way of the work; there is less daylight around, there can be heavy mist on the hills and so on. But luckily the guests we have been seeing are all a bunch of pretty good guys and they know what to do. They know what we expect of them and we get on fine together.

This shooting of the hinds goes on right through the winter, up until the middle of February. In between times we have the odd pheasant-shoot. It is not just a case of having to attend them; you actually quite enjoy it sometimes, because it is a day out for the boys of the glen, you are getting work for your dogs, and you are meeting some of the other keepers, who are friends. Basically, you just have to get up a bit earlier to get down the glen. After all, it's eight miles down before we actually hit the main road, and then we travel on to wherever the shoot is going to be, whether at Blair Castle or Dunkeld or somewhere like that.

But when we get home again it is back to the hinds and, as I have said, that is an on-going job right through to the middle of February. We may well shoot anything up to three or four hundred of them. One winter a few years ago we were averaging eight deer a day for sixty-five days; we shot over five hundred beasts in that spell. There was a good reason for it too: there was a large accumulation of deer on the ground, the weather was very, very bad, and the poor deer were actually little more than skin and bone.

And now, of course, we see the benefit of controlling deer numbers. We can see it paying off, because we are getting heavier beasts, the calves are much bigger, the hinds are in better condition, which means that they can have healthier young. It all comes back to one thing – keeping the numbers down so that there is more food on the hill for them.

Sometimes people wonder if we have much use for dogs when it comes to the hinds, and I would like to say that we don't really use dogs that much. A deer-stalker in general doesn't need a gamedog for general use. But there are always foxes about; most deer-forests have grouse and ptarmigan on them, and quite a few have sheep, so in actual fact a dog is a useful thing to have around. It is a nice sort of thing to have anyway, and I think it is fair to say that most stalkers and gamekeepers would have a few dogs: maybe a labrador, a spaniel, and of course terriers.

My own preference is a black labrador. I have had brown ones, yellow ones and black ones, and it's the black that I like best of all. I have also had spaniels and, though they are good enough on the hill, they are more suited to pheasant-shoots. I like the spaniel well enough – but I would prefer the labrador.

I try to interest the trainees in dogs, though sometimes they

Tired labrador at the end of a day's shoot

seem to wonder if a dog is really a necessity for a gamekeeper. Well, it is. A keeper should have a dog, he really should have his own one. And so should a trainee keeper. He can learn a little about training it, with help from an experienced man. Obviously, a trainee won't know everything about teaching a dog, and getting a dog off on the wrong foot is a dangerous thing. Because once a dog learns a bad habit, it can take a very long time to get rid of it. It takes a long time to train a dog properly, but only two minutes to spoil it – and you don't want that.

OCTOBER

We always have a good number of dogs around the place, some old and some young. Take Sooty, for instance – he is an older dog. In fact, he has just got cataracts in his eyes. I haven't had time to take him down to the vet yet, but in the next week or two I will take him there and see what they can do.

Sooty is the great, great, great grandson of my first-ever dog, which was a very good one who came from another keeper I knew. I got him as a pup, and just kept the strain going with different bitches. I always keep forgetting his age, but I think Sooty is somewhere about the nine-years-old mark. He is a great dog, very obedient and knows his job backwards. I have only once had a fright with him, though it was pretty hair-raising at the time. We were shooting pheasants, and Sooty saw this bird being shot and falling beyond the edge of a steep bank on the river. Well, it was steeper than he thought! He just took off and went straight over the edge of the rock and landed in the water about fifty or sixty feet below.

I thought that was it, and by the time I had scrambled down there was no sign of him. I didn't know if he had landed on the rocks, landed in the water or where he had landed – there was no sign of him, he had just totally disappeared, and I was really sick with worry. I searched for him, whistled for him, but there was nothing to be seen of him, and I thought he was gone for good.

I actually thought I would never see him again. But about two hours later – by this time we were away at another shoot – I saw this poor, bedraggled thing come trailing up the road, and it was Sooty. I must admit he didn't have the pheasant he had gone after, but at least he had come back. And I suppose it was a good thing for him, in the long run. When he goes to the edge of a really steep precipice now, he thinks twice – because he got a hell of a fright, and so did I as well.

He is still fit and healthy. He loves to get out for a run around, and he still picks up pheasants. He still goes to the grouse too. He is an old friend as well as a workmate. Being a keeper, especially a single-handed one, can sometimes be quite lonely. I mean, a man can go for weeks and hardly see another soul, so you can get pretty close to your dogs.

But Sooty is getting old now, and you always have to have a

Carn Liath from Loch Moraig

young dog coming on to replace the old one that will be retiring sooner rather than later. So I have Peel; he is just around the one-year-old mark. I got him from a friend of mine. He has a very good, very long pedigree, and he is a very clever, strong dog. That means he can be taught and trained to work all day without having to take a rest.

I have had no problems with him at all. I have had him out with the pheasants and I am very pleased with him. I have a very good friend who is an expert dog-trainer, and she managed to get some training into him before he came to me. Next season he will be working on the hill. I amn't saying that Sooty will be retired at that point, mind you. But Peel is definitely on the go now. He always jumps into the Land-Rover – he loves being driven around in it. He can jump a fence at the snap of a finger; he sits when he is told, and is coming along fine.

But as I say, it takes a long time to train them, and a very short time to ruin them. If they want to run after a rabbit – well, they are off in a split second. And when they do that there's trouble. I mean, they could run right into the middle of a pheasant-shoot. Or they could take off after a hare on the hill when you are shooting grouse, and if they do that you won't see them for the rest of the day. Luckily, it doesn't happen at the moment, but I have had it happen.

Now, possibly I did the wrong thing in getting young dogs. An older dog would be a better thing for most gamekeepers, especially when they are starting off with sheep in a big way. An older dog understands what you do, and he also helps you to understand how the sheep are going to behave when you go to work with them.

Another important friend, dog-wise, is the fox-terrier. There are various types, but I like the black ones; they seem to be a wee bit hardier and better at their job than the others.

One of my terriers is Deke; he is a wee dog, a black one. He lets you know if there is anyone about the glen at all. He is high up in the kennel and he watches up the glen and down the glen and he barks at everybody that arrives in the place. When Deke came, he just sort of took over the whole place as if it were his own. He works very hard and always lets you know if there is a fox down the hole.

And that is obviously the most important thing for a terrier to do. You can go to each den and see marks, but you need the terrier to make sure for you that there is a fox inside. He goes down the hole and sniffs around and, if there is something there, he lets you know about it. As soon as he starts barking, you know there is a fox down in there somewhere.

Deke is a fly wee character too. He goes down, he barks loud and long, and then he slips back out and sits down beside me, waiting for the fox to come out. And when it does, it gets shot. It is all very humanely done, a lot better than the snares and traps of thirty years ago.

Deke's workmate is called Buster – about the same size, not too high in the leg so he can get down into the fox holes, rock cairns and so on, and he does his job just as a fox-terrier should.

I have one slightly larger called Sparky, and he can sniff them out in rock cairns, but he is a wee bit longer in the leg. He will also run off a bit, and of course a headstrong terrier is something that is not very useful, even though he always does come back. Sparky is a character by himself. When I got him he had actually been a working dog right from the start, and when we get dogs they have to be working dogs because pets are not what are needed on a sporting estate.

And of course you couldn't exactly work sheep without dogs around the place. Around the end of October we usually give the hill a rest, what you might call a week's grace, a week of peace for all the deer on it. We gather our sheep for market. We dip them, take the lambs away from the mothers, and take them off to the sales. There are various sorts of dip, but they all help to keep insects and the like off the sheep over the winter, and it also helps to put a good protective coating on their fleeces. It is helpful for them in wintertime, and usually lasts right through to the spring.

Also, we will be looking at starting to feed the sheep, because frost and snow won't be far away by now. There will still be grass around but you have to top up with hay. The tup, that's the ram, is put out at the start of November, and it is obviously important that the ewes are in good condition to accept him, or the lambs born the following spring won't be in such a condition as they should be.

View of Glen Fender from the lower reaches of Beinn a'Ghlo

Of course, the ewes have had the whole of the summer to get strong and healthy, but we can get a very wet time in October, which brings down their general condition. So we have to feed them, usually from the last days of October, or more likely the early days of November. Whenever it is necessary, basically.

Because by the end of October, we really are thinking about the sort of weather we will soon be facing. So we put feed into the feed-boxes, a bit of hay and, later on, feed-pellets which contain concentrated grass, vitamins and goodness knows what else. Because when a blizzard blows up, and that can happen any time in the winter, the sheep need to be in good condition.

It only takes twenty minutes for them to get covered over in really heavy snow, and obviously this is where a good dog comes in very handy. Mind you, sheep can be surprisingly clever: they can be caught out, but if they are used to you feeding them all you have to do is call out two or three times and they will come running.

But at the back of everyone's mind is the prospect of bad weather arriving early. We have to prepare snow-ploughs, and make sure that we have antifreeze in all the vehicles. We have to have enough coal, wood chopped up into logs, and kindling for the fire in the morning, because the frost can get down as low as twenty-four degrees. I am not saying it happens every year, but it can happen, so we have to be ready to fight it, and be as self-sufficient as possible.

I suppose we are all like big kids at first, looking forward to a bit of snow. But after a few weeks it doesn't seem to be so funny. And it's hard on the animals. The weather really does take the goodness off them. It takes the fat right off the deer, and they use up all their energy.

It's hard on them – it's hard on us too. And with the winter hardly started, it is a very long way to the next spring.

The Story of Keepering –
the Way it Was

Between the period in which Scrope, Prince Albert and Farquharson stalked Glen Tilt in their several ways, and the day
of the late twentieth-century stalker, the Highland sporting estate
underwent many changes.

At first those changes were slow. But when Landseer's pictures and
Victoria's visits to Balmoral publicized deer-hunting in the Highlands
and made it distinctly fashionable, a horde of southern aristocrats and
industrialists was soon on its way north.

The accumulation of extraordinary amounts of disposable income
made possible the rentals, purchase of leases and wholesale acquisition
of estates. A decline in the profitability of sheep-farming meant that
many estates were actively for sale. And the expansion of the railway
network opened up the Highlands to this new breed of tourist: north
from Perth to Inverness in 1863, to Strome Ferry and the west in 1870,
and north again to Wick and Thurso four years later.

A few years afterwards Glasgow was joined with Fort William. To
win permission to build the line across part of the Corrour Forest, the
railway company was required to construct a station exclusively for the
forest's owner, along with the assurance that it would never close as
long as the family owned the estate.

The explosion in interest, when it came, was remarkable. While
Scrope still stalked Tilt, the Earl of Malmesbury (who had been offered
the sporting rights to one large estate for just £25) famously remarked
that *'At that time a stranger could fish and shoot over almost any part of
the Highlands without interruption, the letting of the "ferae naturae" being
unknown to their possessors'*.

But within a decade all had changed. In the words of Robert Somers,
'A deer-forest is beginning to be considered a necessary appendage of an
estate. If it wants that, it wants dignity; and forests, accordingly, are
introduced in much the same spirit as powdered wigs and four-wheeled
carriages at the beginning and the end of the last century'.

On the eve of Victoria's first visit to the Highlands, there were twenty-
eight deer-forests in operation. By 1870 an additional thirty-seven had
been formed. If shepherds, tenant farmers and the settlements of original

183

inhabitants were cleared to make way for them, vast sums were spent first on the preparation of the estates and then on their management as deer-forests and grouse-moors. Fences, butts, roads and drainage were themselves expensive; lodges were very expensive indeed.

Most cost between £10 000 and £20 000 – one cost its owner £40 000 and another as much as £70 000. There was naturally expenditure, too, on the estate employees. In the early years of the century the head forester at Atholl cost the estate £24 in cash, along with meat, grazing, clothes and free house. An under-keeper made do on a little over £6 a year; less exalted casual workers were to be had for a fraction of that.

But by the second part of the century wages had risen. Labourers, apprentices and casual hill-men were still paid very little, but the shooting tenants and owners made sure that they paid their head keepers and under-keepers very well, at least compared to average wages in the locality. In 1850, for instance, £45 was the total cost of one head keeper; by 1863 it was up to £54. Three years later an under-keeper could be had for £30. In 1872 £74 was the price of a head stalker; by 1888 the figure was up to £80 per year.

But the keepers and stalkers had their own price to pay for their wages. The keeper occupied in local society an ambiguous role that would certainly last well into the twentieth century. He was, after all, the landlord's chief custodian of the game – and policeman, too, should that game attract local scrutiny. He was also expected to know very exactly indeed his place in the social order.

As one idealized account from the late 1870s would have the reader believe, the typical keeper lived in a cottage bounded by a well-tended kitchen garden, kennels, ferret hutches and sundry sheds furnished with (by then illegal) man-traps. His favourite rifle, recently converted to a breech-loader (and usually a gift from a gentleman 'rifle') hung in its favourite place; his eldest son, meantime, would be out on the estate learning his ancestral trade.

And at the bosom of this idyllic household we find his good wife, 'whose manners', according to Richard Jefferies, 'from occasional contact with the upper ranks – the ladies from the great house sometimes look in for a few minutes to chat with so old a servant of the family – are above what are usually found in her station'.

Of course, these were the days when the sporting press could carry earnest letters on the complex subject of 'class distinctions in the hunting field'. There was much concern about what constituted a proper gratuity. At 1904 prices, a hundred brace of grouse was recommended as worth a tip of 50p, a day's stalking £1, and a week's stalking £2.

The Story of Keepering – the Way it Was

> The trap is almost precisely similar to the common rat-trap or gin still employed to destroy vermin, but greatly exaggerated in size, so that if stood on end it reaches to the waist or above. The jaws of this iron wolf are horrible to contemplate – rows of serrated projections which fit into each other when closed, alternating with spikes a couple of inches long, like tusks. They seem to snap together with a vicious energy, powerful enough to break the bone of the leg; and assuredly no man ever got free whose foot was once caught by these terrible teeth. The trap could be chained to its place if desired; but as a matter of fact a chain was unnecessary, for no man could possibly drag this torturing clog along.
>
> Richard Jefferies, *The Gamekeeper at Home*

And the keeper's duties were often just as strictly defined. In many ways they were already much as they would be in later years. With regard to the gamebird moor, for example, the keeper was expected to ensure that the heather was burnt sensibly, that the water supply was attended to, that vermin were strenuously suppressed (and ditto poachers), that the birds were fed as appropriate in hard weather (stooks of unthreshed corn), that old cocks were destroyed in autumn, and that from time to time new blood was introduced to the breeding stock.

Plantations had also to be attended to, sheep numbers controlled, land improved with lime as necessary, and wire or iron fences 'bushed' with vegetation, so that the birds might see and avoid them.

The head keeper would also, of course, be expert in the procedures of shooting grouse, whether being driven to flight by dogs or a line of beaters forcing the birds down on to waiting guns at the butts (which were to be at all times clean and dry). And once in the forest, he would be a master of the stalking art. He would know never to stalk downwind, and that he should always endeavour to stalk downhill (for the deer seldom look uphill).

He would know without thinking that he should approach with the sun at his back, remember that deer in general move upwind when they are feeding, and be familiar with their movements relative to weather: as high and remote as possible in good weather, as low and sheltered in bad.

And – among a host of other things, not least associated with the deference due to a visiting sportsman – he should be aware that on very

Of the principal birds found in the Blair Atholl area the following are the collective noun forms:

Crows;		Grouse;	
carrion	*hover*	large group	*pack*
Ducks; in		Hawks	*cast*
flight	*team*	Magpies	*tiding*
Ducks; a pair	*brace*	Partridges	*covey*
Ducks;	*flush*	Pheasants	*nye*
a brood		Pigeons	*flight*
Eagles	*convocation*	Plovers	*congregation*
Geese	*gaggle*	Ravens	*unkindness*
Geese;		Woodcock	*fall*
in flight	*skein*		
Grouse;			
family	*brood*		

Wildlife Ranger's Handbook (Forestry Commission, 1985)

windy days, for reasons unknown, deer will dash all over the glen without warning.

Thus served by armies of similarly skilled retainers, the deer-forest boom of the late nineteenth century showed little sign of slowing down.

Indeed, after 1870, when there were already sixty-five in operation, the boom accelerated. Eleven were formed in the next five years, another five by 1880, and an astonishing twenty-three in the five years to 1885. The total of 104 forests encompassed something like two million acres of the Scottish north. Even then, the boom was unfinished: thirteen more forests joined the roll in the next decade, another sixteen by the turn of the century, and at least twenty more by 1912.

None of this expansion went without a great deal of political controversy. From the early 1880s small subsistence tenants, inspired by the Land League in Ireland, had been agitating for land reform, an agitation first brought to national attention by the journalist Alexander Gow most famously in the *Dundee Advertiser*. Forests were raided and game openly destroyed; a royal commission led to much-demanded land reform, while in the early 1890s a further commission examined the deer-forest question in the northern counties (but not in Perthshire) with a view to returning some of the land to popular agricultural use.

The landlords fought back. In 1909 the forthcoming eighth Duke of Atholl invited critics (among them Gow) to visit Glen Tilt. The visitors agreed that it was not suitable for agricultural purposes. Shortly afterwards, yet another government inquiry found that around three and a half million acres were under deer – about one-fifth of the entire land area of Scotland.

And in 1913 no less a critic than Lloyd George (whose first-ever political meeting in Wales had been addressed by the Irish Land Leaguer Michael Davitt) was also under fire from Scottish landlords. He had fiercely attacked deer-forests as a waste of agricultural land. The Duke of Sutherland, among others of his kind, found the attack a 'vicious' one. Further controversy, clearly on the way, was, however, to be interrupted – without apparent warning.

Throughout the early summer of 1914 the sporting press was waxing lyrical about the *'wonderful killing power'* of the new .22 rifle, and noting that while the previous year had been a disaster for grouse, everything was now set fair on the moors. The *Field* reported excellent prospects in Glen Tilt, and its end-July edition carried a full-cover picture of Walter Winans competing at Bisley for the newly introduced running-boar target.

On 1 August all was still well; the *Field*'s cover featured yachting at Cowes. But a week later, with the caption *'seconds out of the ring'*, it pictured the 25 000-ton *Dreadnought* and complained with an admirable spirit of editorial proportion that *'the mad ambition of an autocrat'* had ruined a season which would otherwise *'have eclipsed all previous records on the moors of the central Highlands'*.

From every corner, keepers and sportsmen dashed to join their territorial or regular units, or to the recruiting stations. Within weeks, game was being sought for field and convalescent hospitals. By Christmas the obituary lists in the sporting press were growing ominously longer.

Some years ago one of the present writers visited a school in the west Highlands and expressed a desire to present a prize to the boy whose powers of observation and definition were the best. Amongst the questions addressed to the class was the one 'What is a gamekeeper?' Answer he received from a bright-eyed, sandy-haired Celt of about ten years of age. 'A big man who goes about in a braw suit of tweeds, with a dog and a gun, and does nothing.'

A. S. Walker and P. J. Mackie, *The Keeper's Book*

The Story of Keepering – the Way it Was

For the forests, the four years of the Great War had many implications. Demand, of course, collapsed; maintenance disappeared; the vixen and her cubs patrolled the hills at will; herds were culled (16 000 head in 1917) in the cause of feeding the fighting and civilian populations.

And when it had all finished, two decades of retrenchment were introduced. On the face of it, owners, factors, sportsmen, stalkers and keepers returned (or did not return) from France, Flanders and the other theatres of war and took up where they had left off. But, as with so much else, the old spirit of things had gone; the old zest for slaughter had, perhaps, somewhat diminished. A new sensitivity to considerations of class and culture might even have entered the long-established equations of the social order.

There was, perhaps, a wider appreciation of one comment, to the effect that

> ... the Highlander is a born hunter, and the descendant of a long line of hunters. His ancestors having been brought up under the clan system, 'blue' blood runs in his veins ... the pride and exigencies of race which have confined the Highlander's instincts to hunting and fighting also assert themselves in a marked way in his relations to his master. If the latter is 'the laird', one of a line of fifty Campbells, a hundred Macintoshes or a thousand Grants, then the Highlander is a much more satisfactory workman than if his master is a 'Sassenach', or comes of a branch of what he still virtually regards as an alien people.

Such niceties aside, however, the day-to-day management of the estate went on as it had done in the past. Trainees were required to be keenly interested in natural history; they were to be weaned as kennel-boys and quickly taught to handle ferrets for rabbiting and to understand their distinct peculiarities of personality and behaviour. The management of ponies should follow; then the control of heather, and the duties of draining, fencing and planting.

Only then should the apprentice be introduced to weaponry – at first the use of snares, traps and nets; then, initially as an observer, of firearms. The keeper would also have an intimate knowledge of the law as it related to the poaching of birds, deer and salmon. In the case of salmon he would know all about the use of poisons and explosives, of ring and gill nets, of traps, lights and fires, snares, rippers, gaffs, leisters and otters; and the scores of other ways of taking salmon which have been popularly devised over the centuries.

But though some superficial things remained unchanged, other great

> *In selecting ponies for hill work, whether for carrying panniers, deer, or men, the truism must be stated that the main point to observe is to select ponies that can climb. They should never be Lowland born or bred, and their chief qualifications should be strength and sureness of foot. They should possess these qualifications along with that of being good climbers, at the expense of speed and style, which should never be looked for. They should not be too small – size and substance is what is needed. The shoulders should have a moderate slope – this ensures sureness of foot – and breadth of loin and substance of bone should be demanded. In working the ponies they should be allowed as much as possible to have their own way, and to pick out their own stepping ground. They should be allowed to go slowly. How often have we seen a pony fall, simply because the rider or the leader would persist in jerking its head backwards.*
>
> A. S. Walker and P. J. Mackie, *The Keeper's Book*

changes were slowly making themselves apparent. The Great War had, in a way that was not immediately noticeable, significantly broken the power of pre-war Britain and of the wealthy classes who had enjoyed the prosperity that that power had brought. The twenties that followed were a decade of post-war gloom, and the thirties in their turn introduced the Depression and rearmament.

The upshot was further war and the beginning of the end of Britain as an imperial power. Unlike 1914, the last year of the thirties allowed a short grouse season, but the autumn stags were to be left in peace. As the *Field* announced in its first September editorial, 'We are writing this on 1 September. It is now three o'clock in the afternoon, and the office radio has just notified us that the King has signed the General Mobilization Order.'

✤ NOVEMBER ✤

By now we are well into the autumn and beginning to get ready for the main tasks that have to be attended to before the weather gets really bad and the days very short next month. So November is basically for two main jobs – culling the hinds and getting on with the pheasant-shooting.

You'll remember that the stag-stalking stops at the end of the third week in October, and after that we give the hill a rest for a week or so, give the herds a break and a bit of a chance to settle down, while we get on with one or two other things around the place. For one thing, we use the time to gather sheep, take the lambs away and send them off to market. And we also do a bit of dipping the sheep as well, so that takes about a week or so.

But after the deer have had their fortnight's grace and the hill has calmed down a bit, then we are off after the hinds as hard as we can go. After their wee rest things have calmed down a bit on the hill and, though the deer are always on the alert, it makes the job that bit easier for us.

And so we get started into the hinds, usually with a few guests to give us a hand. We have to strike a balance here between the wishes of the guests and the needs of the professional stalkers, and I am pleased to say we seem to manage this balance pretty well. I suppose it would be easier, or at least faster, if we did all the culling ourselves – but then, it is nice to be able to take guests to the hill, and see them enjoy their sport. And it breaks up the main job for us too.

Most of these guests, perhaps I should say all of them, are very interested and are very good on the hill – and I think we tend to take more care in picking deer when we have these guests with us. Of course, before they arrive we have to find out who they are, how many days they would like to come for, and then we get them booked in at a local hotel or guest-house.

Anyway, when they arrive we explain to them what the situation is, explain that we are not going out on the hill for any sort of wholesale slaughter. We tell them that we are out to pick off selected hinds and calves, to take out the old, the sick, those unlikely to survive the coming winter, for the benefit of the deer population as a whole.

And then, of course, we get some target-practice done, before any of the guests goes near the hill. We see what type of rifle they have, check their ammunition, make sure that everything is legal and above-board in terms of shooting hinds. A lot of the guests are farmers from down south and have done plenty of shooting on a fairly regular basis, so that's not a problem.

But low-country shooting – well, they don't tend to have red-deer herds, and most of the shooting is for smaller land-game like roe-deer or foxes, and their rifles are sometimes on the low-calibre side for red-deer hinds. So now and again they need a heavier-calibre weapon, and we normally get that fixed up in the first few hours after they arrive. So off we go to the target-practice, and we like to think that after a bit of work there they are capable of hitting a five-inch bull at 150 yards. That is quite a reasonable range to be firing at a hind, and it is perfectly reasonable for us to expect our guests to be able to manage it.

So after that, we can head for the hill, taking care to remember that some of these guys are maybe just not as fit as we are. That's understandable – we're working in Glen Tilt all year round, whereas people more used to the flatter land of the south just don't get the same chance to be as fit as we are. Mind you, there are quite a few of them who can give us the odd surprise, too, when it comes to fitness, that's for sure!

So once we've got the target-practice up to standard and out of the way, we head for the hill – on foot or by Land-Rover, whichever is the easier, depending on where we are headed. We tell them where we are going and show them where the deer are. Most of the time the guests are very clued up about this sort of thing; they know how to act and how to react on the hill. If you stop, they stop; they know how to spy with binoculars and so on. Sometimes,

191

Maurice Dow, head keeper at Tulliemet

of course, we get the occasional novice who doesn't really know the first thing about the job, and that is when it is up to us to assess them very quickly and put them at ease.

For instance, we sometimes have a good idea if someone is going to suffer from buck-fever. And obviously we don't want anyone shooting at a hind and failing to kill it outright: we don't ever want to see a beast wounded by a shot. If that happens, it has to be trailed and shot as soon as possible, which makes a lot of extra work for everyone, quite apart from any consideration of the poor wounded beast.

After all, we are on the hill at this time of the year not primarily to provide sport but to cull the hinds, so it is our job to point out the beasts that need to be shot, and get on with that main job.

That's why the hind-shooting is much less expensive than the stags, roughly about a third of the price, indeed. So the guests pay for the shooting, and of course they can take away with them what they have shot – they pay extra for that, depending on what the weight of the venison comes in at. We skin the beast more or less

---

Irish guest on a shoot

on the spot and then weigh it in front of the guests, and charge them according to the going rate for venison at that particular time of the year.

We have some people who have been coming for years and years, and others who just phone up out of the blue and ask whether they can have a go. And the newcomers enjoy it just as much as the old hands; they enjoy not just the shooting but the day out as well, the scenery in the glen and so on. We tell them stories about the glen, something about its history, they see a bit of off-road driving, which can be quite exciting if you are not used to it.

Gralloching a deer

NOVEMBER

A lot depends on the weather, of course. Later on in the year especially, it can be a different story and we need to be kitted out in winter gear. Sometimes we might be wearing our camouflage-white snow shoes, which can be a big help when it comes to stalking in snowy conditions. And the weather also affects the deer, naturally. If the weather is poor and the deer are wet and tired, they can be pretty lethargic, and stalking them is relatively easy. But in better weather conditions they can all be fit and strong. If they have had a long run of good weather and plenty of feeding, they will be on the alert at all times.

So when that is the case, you might just manage to shoot one or two in a day – and that is your day finished, because the rest of the herd take off into the distance, and you don't always have the daylight to go after them and get home in time. Remember, they don't just run a hundred yards or so and stop there for the rest of the day. They will maybe run that distance and stop for a few moments: that's the chance to get in another shot or two. But it depends if we have guests with us or not.

If it's myself with the rifle, well I know exactly what beast or beasts to shoot at, and I can do that very quickly. But with a guest it is a different story. When you are trying to tell someone which beast to pick from a herd of maybe two hundred, it is a different matter altogether. That makes things a lot slower, and most times the deer are away and over the skyline. So that tends to be the end of the day, unless we go on to another herd and take some out of that.

And when we do call an end to shooting, the beasts have to be bled and gralloched. We show them how to do that, and some are very interested – and next time round, they will have a go at it themselves. And then there are others who don't want to have anything to do with it – they're quite happy to pull the trigger and shoot the beast. But to be honest, that's the easy part of the job.

The hard part is getting the kill back to base. For instance, if you are struggling with the dead weight of a hind on a steep slope covered with ice, it can be very dangerous. You can't always use ponies or quad bikes in conditions like that, so it's manpower rather than horsepower. A good friend of mine uses what he calls his pocket-winch, just a bit of rope tied around the head and the legs of the beast. It's just a case of dragging the kill behind you – and sometimes that could be for as long as a mile or more. If there is snow on the ground the beast acts like a sledge which is great on level ground, but it can be dangerous going downhill, because it can take off and knock the legs from under you. You have to be very careful on the hill at times like that. But we all take a tumble sooner or later; it is just about impossible not to.

I have mentioned instep crampons earlier, and these are the sort of conditions where they come in very handy indeed. This is when they come into their own. If you are having to drag a deer they give you a great grip, and are really an important safety factor. We all use them when conditions are like that.

So after a while of dragging we can get back to a vehicle, and in due course get the day's kill back to base and the larder. We get them on to the bench and hang them up and clean them out – get them ready for the game-dealer. Depending on what the weather is doing, we may find ourselves doing three days' shooting and then load up the Land-Rovers and take all the carcasses down the glen, down to the end of our track, eight miles of it, and rendezvous with the game-dealer who is waiting there with his van.

He picks them up from us, though sometimes, if we deliver them to him, he will add on an extra two or three pence a pound. But really we don't have an awful lot of time to do that because we like to get out and get on with the job of culling. It is often six days a week, certainly five and a half unless the weather gets in the way – and with one or other of the boys away at college we tend to be a bit short-handed anyway. The college has been very kind and lets the young lads stay with us during the August–September–October shooting season, but now you can probably have two of them away for five or six weeks at a time.

So we normally have our hands fairly full at the time of the hind-culling. And of course that means we are also sometimes a bit short-handed at the pheasant-shooting. Because apart from the hinds, that's the other main occupation at this time of the year: shooting the pheasants on the low ground.

We go down and help out at the shoots down there. Of course, it's a completely different sort of shooting to what we do up the glen. It is back to the old shotgun, which is a different sort of creature altogether. With a heavy-calibre rifle, you are firing just one projectile at a time, but even though you aren't usually shooting at anything more than a couple of hundred yards, that bullet can travel and be lethal at goodness knows how many miles in the case of some rifles. But the shotgun ... well, the most common calibre is the twelve-bore, which puts out a spread of small lead pellets, so in a way it's a lot easier to hit what you are aiming at, though the range of the gun is very short compared to the rifle. Of course, shooting at fast-flying birds isn't exactly a job for the rifle!

It's normally the same gun as we employ for the grouse, though probably you would find that a different size of shot is used. Obviously, you want to use heavier shot for some sorts of birds – in other words, there are less lead pellets in each cartridge, but each one is larger and has greater stopping power. So though we might well use sizes six and seven for grouse, we could find ourselves using fives and sixes for pheasants.

So you might have, say, 450 pellets in some sizes of cartridges, but of course you don't hit the target with all of them. As the pellets leave the barrel of the gun they spread out in a cone shape with a six-foot spread, so that at a normal sort of range you probably only hit the target with about seven or eight pellets. It is the penetration and shock of these few pellets which actually do the killing. So obviously it is very important that you never shoot at animals or birds which are too far away, which is something that people can do now and again. But it is very important to shoot at the correct range for the gauge of shotgun you are using and the type of ammunition you have loaded into it.

It's maybe worth mentioning, by the way, that the day of lead pellets is just about done. Lead is bad news for the natural environment, so I think that in the near future you might find lead being made illegal. So there will have to be some sort of alternative available – steel, or something like that. We don't really know what it will be, because it is still being worked on. We can only hope that it is as effective as lead, and at the same time does less harm to the environment.

The shooting itself is a sort of day out for the keepers. They have spent a lot of the rest of the year raising the pheasants, feeding them every day, guarding them against predators, looking after them like children basically. For most keepers, really, their heart is in bringing them up. If something happens to the young pheasants they get pretty annoyed: so they get well looked after. But by now the time has come round for what you could call the final stage, when the birds are all grown up and they are put out into cover ready for the shoots.

In a way it is roughly similar to a grouse-shoot, but this time you have, say, eight or nine guns placed at the end of the wood or the field in which the pheasants are.

But unlike your line of guns, who walk the moor and drive up the grouse from the heather before them, this time the beaters drive down the birds onto the waiting guns. The keepers, lads, dogs, assistants, could be half a mile away or maybe half that distance. The guns are perhaps sixty or seventy yards apart, stretched out over four or five hundred yards.

And then the beaters, with their dogs and sticks, proceed very slowly towards them, flushing out pheasants, woodcock, partridges or whatever is there. When the beaters get to within a hundred yards or so of the guns, the head keeper will blow his horn, and that means the guns will stop shooting or only shoot at birds that have already flown past them.

Obviously, that is a safety precaution – and, for the same reason, nowadays the guns aren't allowed to shoot at any ground-game that may have been flushed by the beaters, the likes of hares, rabbits, foxes and so on. Pellets can always bounce off the ground, especially if it is frozen, or ricochet off something solid enough – plus, of course, there are plenty of people and dogs in the immediate vicinity anyway.

And, of course, away at the back of the guns are the people we call the pickers. They are some of the most important people we have on this sort of shoot, positioned maybe three or four hundred yards beyond the guns. Sometimes, naturally, a bird isn't shot down dead but is what we call peppered – that is, wounded, but still able to fly a few hundred yards before it comes down. So the pickers, sometimes one picker per gun, are stationed with good dogs, probably spaniels or labradors, and their job is to watch out for birds like that, and when they see one come down the dogs will retrieve it at once.

The keeper's shoot – the last pheasant shoot of the season

NOVEMBER

We usually have three drives in the morning, and then we have a quick lunch – what you might call a walking lunch. At this time of the year the nights are really drawing in, and it is getting dark any time after half-past three, so you have basically got a very short afternoon. So in the last few years we have just had a quick snack, and then have another two or three drives, and call it a day before it gets dark.

At this point everyone goes into the bothy or they retire to the local pub and have a bar meal. The beaters can go to a shed or a barnhouse if we're on a farm, and everyone can still get home in reasonable time.

There's no question this is the best way of doing it, and not just because it is convenient for everyone. It also means that any pheasants which were flushed during the day and were not shot can come back to their own normal roosting area. Obviously, they won't come back when shooting is still going on, but if you leave the last bit of light for those that have escaped then they have a chance to make their way home, rather than roost in some strange place where a fox or whatever could get them during the night.

And it means, of course, that they are back where they should be next morning. They are a wee bit wary at first, but you whistle at them and feed them, and by the time a fortnight has passed you are ready for another shoot.

And that, pretty much, is the way we get through November – culling the hinds, and taking the benefit of all the work we have put in earlier in the year on rearing the pheasants.

By the end of the month – well, we have had a pretty tiring month. But the end of the year is approaching, we're just a few weeks away from the festive season once again, and that gives everyone in the glen something to look forward to, especially the younger ones. And of course we are all hoping that the weather will be reasonable, that we'll be able to get up and down the glen without too much trouble. It doesn't always happen like that – but it doesn't stop us hoping, either!

Waterfall on the River Tilt in winter

Atholl:
the Modern Sporting Estate

In the last two decades or so, a number of considerations have altered significantly the nature of many a Highland sporting estate. In this period of change, the Atholl estate has been something of a beacon of continuity in an otherwise uncertain landscape. But even for Atholl the uncertainties ensure that the estate, and its community, is not guaranteed to retain in the future the sort of past it has for so long enjoyed.

In this respect the most critical issue is ownership. In terms of land ownership on a wider national scale, the Highlands are still mainly in the hands of sometimes very large estates. A little over two decades ago (and more recent figures are not easily available) two and a half million acres of the Scottish landmass were state-owned, mostly by the Forestry Commission. The remaining sixteen and a half million acres were in private hands, and some of these were very large hands indeed.

Over the course of these twenty-odd years, many sporting estates in the Highlands have changed hands and altered in nature.

On the west coast, for instance, the peninsular deer-forest of Knoydart, after repeated buying and selling, was finally disposed of by its southern property-developer owner in a number of separate lots, now generally in foreign and anonymous ownership. Closer to Atholl, an American divorce settlement was the leading factor in the destiny of the Mar Lodge estate. And the Morar estate, again on the west coast, came into the ownership of the theatrical impresario, Cameron

> Landowners can fall into a proprietorial attitude to land which is logically absurd; the cliché that no one owns land, but that they only look after it for a while, is completely true. Our islands are too small for parcels of land to be carved out and protected for the purposes of solitude.
>
> Michael Wigan, *Stag at Bay*

Mackintosh. In the ownership of the Frasers of Lovat since the late eighteenth century, it had to be sold to cover debts following the untimely death of the Master of Lovat.

But none of these considerations have complicated the picture in Atholl, where the record shows gradual social change underpinned by a marked continuity in the ownership and management of the estate.

In the mid-1950s the parish was once again described by the local minister (who updated his report a handful of years later) in *The Third Statistical Account of Scotland*. The Rev. Cameron wrote at somewhat lesser length than his predecessors, but even so it is clear that, as might be expected, the physical nature of Atholl had not changed significantly. Nor had the story of its human population (other than having extended itself into the age of wire-less sound broadcasting).

In 1961 the population was chiefly housed in the villages of Blair Atholl, *'the Calvine-Struan group five miles west along the main Inverness road and little clachans at Old Blair, Pitagowan, Old Bridge of Tilt, Trinafour and Fincastle'*. The population, which had been 2848 in 1801, had by 1961 fallen to 1458. Of that total, *'10% have their origins outside the county, 40% within the county, and 50% within the parish'*.

Education, particularly at the primary level, was well catered for. There were primary schools at Blair Atholl (a three-teacher school with a roll of eighty-five) and others at Struan, Dalnacardoch, Dalnaspidal, Trinafour and Strathtummel (to which last the pupils at the former Fincastle School had recently transferred). In all, there were around 150 primary-school children in the parish; 'in addition, about 40 are receiving higher education at Pitlochry High School, Breadalbane Academy, Aberfeldy, and in other schools outwith the county'.

The main industry was agriculture, with about thirty-five per cent engaged directly or indirectly in it; *'the estates, forestry, keepering and maintenance employ about a quarter'*. The largest jolt to district employment had been the recent closure of railway works. By 1961 diesel-fired engines were replacing the less-powerful steam locomotives that had long served the Highland rail routes. British Rail (a state-owned business that ran the national network of track, rolling stock and stations) no longer needed a supply of coal-fuelled engines to help trains over the Drumochter Pass, and seventy-two men had been deployed elsewhere in the network.

Over ninety-five per cent of the population were adherents of the Church of Scotland, and church membership totalled 400. Church-going was 'fair' in the Rev. Cameron's opinion: *'about 15% never go, 30% are regular church-goers, and the rest have occasional visits'*. There was a *'fundamental deep regard'* for the church, which boasted a women's guild, Sunday schools, Bible classes, youth groups and choirs.

In terms of communal activities there were for youngsters scouts, guides and cadets; for older people a Masonic Lodge and a branch of the Women's Rural Institute. And apart from enjoying dancing, whists and concerts, a fair number of parishioners made a weekly visit to the cinema in Pitlochry. Most houses had a radio, and from the new transmission mast at Blair Walker television signals were beamed to the eighty receiving-sets in the village. The general level of health was high; there was no poverty; and the people were kindly, canny and of independent nature.

There were but a few incomers who took *'a few years before becoming involved in the life of the community, and those who do not usually make their stay short'*.

Finally there was no crime to speak of, though poaching was fairly common; *'such poaching for the pot is tolerated by most of the landlords, perhaps out of kindness of heart or the difficulty of making a prosecution'*.

Just over three decades on from 1961, the minister of the parish reported little significant change there.

According to the Rev. James Duncan, the principal change on the economic front was the growth of tourism. Blair Atholl now had two large residential holiday parks, busy from April to October, and of considerable economic clout in the locality. The primary schools at Dalnacardoch, Dalnaspidal, Trinafour and Strathtummel had been closed, while church membership was down to just under 200.

No one visited the cinema in Pitlochry any more: it had closed down.

The general level of health was high, and there was no significant poverty in the district. The local people were still *'kindly, canny and independent by nature'*; though of incomers there were many more, with a considerable number of holiday-homers, or full-time residents who had retired and moved from south of the border to Blair Atholl.

On the population front, the slow decline of the preceding centuries had not been reversed. As the 1991 Census Monitor indicates, the population of that date stood at 906 (of whom just 3.3 per cent claimed a knowledge of the Gaelic language). Over seventy per cent of women were in employment. And while one-fifth of households had no car, one-quarter had two or more cars (testament to the dispersed, rural nature of the parish rather than to any particular wealth on the part of its residents).

But though change there had been, it had nevertheless enjoyed a slow and measured character – arguably because of the continuity of ownership and purpose that the Atholl estate has traditionally enjoyed.

Atholl: the Modern Sporting Estate

> *Because field sports are now politically controversial, politicians and lobbyists choose to close their eyes to the fact that shooting, stalking and fishing provide an annual income running into many millions for Scotland, for which there is no alternative source of revenue with animal husbandry in historic decline. Yet does the government or the public have the stomach to burden the national purse with the huge costs of subsidizing the northern wildernesses, costs now largely borne by private estates? The great misunderstanding by much of the public is that the Highland hills and their wildlife can merely be left to nature and to God. Yet in reality ... the Highlands are a carefully, if invisibly, tended environment. Somebody must pay the bills if we want them to survive.*
>
> Max Hastings, *Daily Telegraph*

But that sort of continuity can not be guaranteed in years to come. The future will depend on the succession to the present duke, on the wealth commanded by his successor, on government policies relating to land use, on European Union rules governing the subsidization of remote agricultural communities, and on estate strategies, which are sometimes by necessity of conflicting character, for the management of Atholl's 130 000 acres.

The present duke, after all, is rather more than a mere custodian of an awful lot of land he just happened to inherit because he was lucky enough to be third cousin to the last owner. His mother was sister to Lord Cowdray, a man worth £350 million, according to the 1990 *Sunday Times Book of the Rich*. (Cowdray's family owned at the same date twenty per cent of the Pearson Group, worth *'around £1.7 billion'*.) Said by the same source to be himself worth £140 million, the duke was born in 1931 and was schooled at Eton and Oxford before inheriting the title of tenth Duke of Atholl at the age of twenty-five.

His interest in matters relating to land management in the Highlands seems proven. A one-time member of the Red Deer Commission and an executive member of the National Trust for Scotland, he was for five years president of the Scottish Landowners' Federation.

But according to the most recent edition of *Who's Who*, the duke is also a director of Westminster Press, BPM Holdings and Pearson Longman – operations whose cash-flows dwarf that of any Highland sporting estate, no matter how large, no matter how developed the spirit may be of ancestral trusteeship for it on the part of its owner.

But the duke is unmarried and approaching pensionable age. Should the day come when resources such as his are not associated with the Atholl estate, then its owner, should he have no external resources to call on, may have to consider it as a strictly business operation – that is, in terms of return on capital value.

Atholl, after all, could in theory be sold on the property market like any other bit of real estate. Would the capital realized by its sale, whether merely banked or otherwise invested, yield more in such circumstances than the estate does now? Would a buyer, as has happened elsewhere in the Highlands, strip out the assets, sell them off in chunks (keeping perhaps just Blair Castle and its policies for himself) and maybe even show a profit on the deal as well?

Of course, though possible, such a course of action seems inconceivable. But the profit-and-loss economics of estate management can

Interviewer: *What happens to the title in future?*
Duke of Atholl: *The title goes to my nearest male relative, who is a South African, and he will inherit it, or his son, whoever outlives the other.*
Interviewer: *And the estate?*
Duke of Atholl: *I would like to see it continue in the same way as I have been able to run it. It will mean whoever has got it in the future will have to have some money.*
Interviewer: *Why?*
Duke of Atholl: *Well, you are never going to make money from a Scottish estate, so you have to be prepared to put some money into it, and I think my nephew will have some money.*
Interviewer: *Isn't the estate profitable?*
Duke of Atholl: *No, it's not.*
Interviewer: *So why do it?*
Duke of Atholl: *We do it because we want to – because we like doing it.*

Interview with the Duke of Atholl

never be overlooked, whatever the nature of its ownership. This holds
good for pretty much every one of the 450 estates (some of them very
small) across which the 250 000 red deer of the Highlands presently
roam. Among them must be counted the Atholl estate. The Forest of
Atholl, after all, turns over cash in terms of deer, grouse and sheep –
but not one of these is a guaranteed income provider.

As Michael Wigan writes in his *Stag at Bay*:

> *The costs of owning deer-forests at prevailing venison and stalking*
> *values are prodigious. Naturally owners are not rushing forward*
> *to announce the scale to which they subsidize their sporting assets,*
> *but it is thought there are no pure deer-forest properties which turn*
> *in a regular annual profit, even ones operating as commercially as*
> *possible. Disadvantaged west-coast forests, possibly dependent on*
> *access by boat, or at the end of long tracks, could cost up to £4*
> *an acre a year, mainstream west-coast forests £3 an acre, and in*
> *the eastern and central Highlands, with the support of revenues*
> *from grouse-moors, the figure might be £2.*

In other words, deer-centred operations in themselves, whether in
terms of stalking income or sale of venison, do not make money. Salmon
and grouse can be better money-spinners (though not all estates boast
their presence in sufficient numbers) – but grouse in particular can
demonstrate catastrophic swings in numbers from year to year.

Wigan repeats what has been long known: '*Grouse-moors are cyclical,*
expensive to manage compared to deer-forests, and they do not unfailingly
produce the goods even when treated to textbook management.'

Salmon, too, are not always the money-makers they can be (though lots
of money has been made by letting and trading in beats and timeshares,
operations which arc of the essence of hard commerce rather than sporting husbandry).

And such money as has in the past been made from sheep will not be
available for much longer. The practice of subsidy is under imminent
sentence of death – and without it no hill-sheep farmer can be expected
to show a profit. As Wigan says: '*With the future of sheep farming in the*
hills at risk from the progressive withdrawal of its subsidy lifeline, the entire
land-use picture may be due to change in the most radical way since large-
scale sheep farming arrived in the Highlands 200 years ago.'

But even if an estate is lucky enough to make a profit on its operations,
or enjoy the subsidy of an independently wealthy owner, it still faces a
range of competing strategies in terms of how it is managed, and in the
context of governmental policy-making over which it has little control.

Atholl: the Modern Sporting Estate

Consider the case of Atholl, for instance. Changes in fashion, fluctuations in disposable income, the availability of more attractive shooting elsewhere, development in long-range transport, the incidence of grouse disease, and any number of other factors could affect the estate economy. Perhaps, at least on paper, it could be afforested. But in this context the interests of commerce and the powerful ecology lobbies do not always coincide.

Nor is Glen Tilt likely to be Scotland's next ski-resort (should there ever be one): development costs, established competition, weight of demand, suitability or otherwise of terrain and uncertainties of weather see to that.

Or perhaps the glen could be left uncared for and entirely uninhabited (though rigorous control over deer numbers would still have to be executed: by whom, in such a context, is not clear). And even if the land were managed in some other way that made economic and/or ecological sense, there would remain two prickly questions.

The first of these is the question of access, for long a controversial one and, as the demands of urban recreation grow, not one that is likely to go away. It has long been a difficult issue but was relatively disguised in earlier times when urban residents could not easily get to the hills and when locals had more sense than to climb mountains for no discernible reason. (And if they were there for a reason, it would not be one they would want anyone in authority to know about.)

Strangely enough, Glen Tilt has historically been at the heart of the question of right of access. Just a few years after Robert Somers visited in the 1840s, a professor of botany at Edinburgh University led a group of students into it, where he was confronted by an angry duke and a party of employees. A row developed. The matter ended in court, which established that there was a right of way up Glen Tilt. The decision was an important one, and it inspired, forty years later, a campaign to establish a statutory right of access to the Scottish hills, though the campaign did not clearly win that objective. (A right of way is a legally recognized right of passage between two points on account of established previous usage. It is an issue separate from that of a general right of access to open countryside.) The issue of access is therefore not an entirely clear one, and increasing public use of the hills is likely to exacerbate rather than quietly resolve the matter.

The second question may be equally controversial. The day is approaching – almost certainly rapidly – when the animal rights movement (and that is the correct word to describe what is a potentially mass phenomenon) will assert itself powerfully. Animal rights supporters have

Atholl: the Modern Sporting Estate

Field sports can cost a lot, though they don't all have to, according to the British Field Sports Society. For the beginner, the first expense would be lessons. The famous Scottish firm of John Dickson (which once sold a stalking-rifle to Queen Victoria as a present for John Brown) runs a shooting-school outside Edinburgh. A lesson costs £53; two or three lessons can render a naturally talented beginner safe and competent with a shotgun. The beginner's gear and own twelve-bore gun, complete with licence, will cost around £200. For a participant in a syndicate, the cost of rough shooting (rabbits, pigeons, the occasional partridge) for a whole season (from August to January) across 700 acres would be just £125 per gun. The very best of rough shooting, including some grouse, might cost £1000 a season. Driven pheasant is more expensive: in a syndicate, eight to ten days' shooting could cost £2000 to £3000 per gun. Hiring a day's commercial shooting on a solo basis, the cost of driven pheasant could range from £12 to £18 per bird shot. Grouse are a lot more expensive: a bird from a top-quality driven-grouse moor would cost £90 – and a shot might expect to down twenty in a day. The average cost of driven grouse, however, is £75 per bird; for walked-up grouse, £30 per bird.

The bill in full	£
Gun (hand-made Purdey)	18 000 and upwards
Gun (average twelve-bore)	750
Gun (Russian Baikal)	110
Rifle (cheaper new)	500
Rifle (top-class)	2000
Boots (cheapest)	10
Waxed jacket and hat (from)	30
Transport	varies
Game ammunition (box of 25)	4
Accommodation	varies
One pheasant	12 – 18
Gratuities	optional
Grouse (per bird)	30 – 90
Hind (one day, one gun)	50 – 100
Stag (one day, one gun)	225

Does anyone have a right to walk unhindered in open countryside in Scotland (as long as they don't invade privacy, damage property or wander on cultivated land)? In Scotland there is a law of trespass. But trespass is a civil rather than criminal matter; and there is no penalty stipulated for the simple act of trespass. A landowner has the right to ask a person to leave his land – but the mere fact of being on private land is not in itself an offence. It is generally recognized that there is a de facto right to roam the hills: in other words the Scots, and their visitors, enjoy a presumption in favour of freedom of access to the Scottish hills. Hence the widely held (if strictly erroneous) view that 'there is no law of trespass in Scotland'.

Material extracted from *Scotland on Sunday*

already campaigned about some marine mammals, a range of domestic pets and a number of intensively farmed animals. They may yet turn their attentions to the red deer.

It matters little that the countryside professional may care as much about wildlife (and know more about its realities) than the generally urban animal rights activist. The latter has a driving principle that animals deserve better treatment from mankind than they have had in the past and continue to get today. That is a reasonable principle with a strong appeal to an urban audience, and it is one that is likely to cast its net ever more widely.

The matter, therefore, is one that land managers in the Highlands will yet have to confront – and sooner, in all likelihood, than later.

For estates and their employees this all means an interesting, complicated and uncertain future. There is, however, one certainty, recognition of which unites everyone concerned with the countryside, from grandest laird to lowliest part-time pony-man – and that is that they are, all of them, custodians of a natural heritage, of a rural environment, which does not, ultimately, look after itself. Should they fail to do that looking after, and resolve in the process the complexities of that responsibility, successor generations will without question be the poorer.

❧ DECEMBER ❧

By this time of the year we're not exactly in a position to pretend that we are anywhere but deep into winter, with all that entails in the way of short, dark days and long, darker nights, and endless trouble with gales, snow-drifts, blizzards and ice.

But the work must go on, so far as we are able to get on with it, and in December, apart from the weather getting in the way, the main outside work is watching and feeding the sheep, keeping the foxes under some sort of control, and of course watching out for hill-climbers who might get into difficulties.

This is very much a time when the foxes' minds are turning to thoughts of mating and the dogs and vixens are running together in pairs. They have sort of established their territory, and it is a good opportunity for us to observe these pairs carefully and see where they might be planning to rear their cubs. Although we are still involved with culling hinds and with pheasant-shoots, this is an excellent time of the year to be out on the hill shooting the foxes: because if we can do it now, it saves us a lot of work having to try to catch up with them later in the spring – though in December the spring seems awful distant when you are up Glen Tilt!

But by the spring we will be busy with lambing, so we get the fox control under way now, and as good a way as any of doing that is to get them by spotlight or night-sight.

Now, I have to emphasize this is not a sport in any way at all. The fox is a lovely creature, to tell you the truth, and way deep down a lot of keepers have a sort of respect for it. But they are savage, ruthless predators – that's their nature, of course, you can't blame them for it. And once you have seen the sort of damage a

Winter sunset, Tulliemet

fox can do to lambs or poultry or whatever, you don't feel so nice about them, believe me. So in no way is it a sport. Lying out half the night on a sub-zero mountainside with a gale blowing around in the pitch dark is nobody's idea of fun, that's for sure.

But we have to get them, and this is the time of the year for it, because weather conditions have forced them down from the high tops. And they aren't down here for nothing; they are here to kill whatever they can get at. And we shoot them at any opportunity. Now and again, what with it being the mating season, we have even got them on what you might call the hop. Not very gentlemanly, I'll admit, but the fox isn't much of a gentleman when it comes to killing, either!

We shoot as many as we possibly can, although we have quite a stretch of ground to cover: eight miles down the way, and another eight miles back into the mountains. Over a whole year we might get twenty or thirty foxes, though that is quite a high count. Some years it will be less, on an occasional year a little more.

As a method of killing the foxes, spotlighting has really only come into use in the last twenty or thirty years. I amn't saying it wasn't done before that, but usually it was poachers who used spotlights to shoot deer. Run a spotlight over a bunch of hinds, say, and you will at once gauge the position of individual beasts by the way their eyes glitter. That way a poacher can put a full beam accurately on to a beast very quickly; and while it is a bit dazed for a few moments with the bright light, then it can be shot. I have even heard of left-handed shots – that is, they use the rifle on their left shoulder instead of the right – firing from the rear near-side passenger seat of a parked car, while the driver shines the torch through the front near-side window.

Of course, this is something which should never be done, shooting deer by spotlight. I have heard of farmers who have had to consider it in desperation, because deer can do terrible damage to crops in just one night. But to do it properly, you should have a permit from the Red Deer Commission. The person who goes out by himself to shoot deer with a spotlight is frowned upon by most sportsmen.

Often enough, the poacher's policy is an indiscriminate one of shoot to kill, to get as many beasts as possible and sell them for as much money as possible. Sometimes they use shotguns, which is a terrible thing to use on a deer – it is really destructive and horrible. I would say that by all means landlords, keepers and policemen should be out to stop that sort of thing. Poachers often shoot at the first beast going, rather than selecting their kill carefully.

He usually fires off his shot as quickly as possible and gets away from the scene of the crime as fast as he possibly can, whether by foot or by car if he is poaching beside a road. Somehow or other, poaching seems to be a draw for some people year after year – at times you would think it was almost hereditary in some families. Why they do it is a mystery at times. You would almost think that for some of them at least it was a kind of way of getting at the landlords, or maybe the law of the land. I suppose some of them do it for the money, but others seem to think it is some sort of sport.

But there are even funnier ones than that. I heard a story the other day, a true story, that two or three strange vans were sighted not too long ago in a glen not too far from here. Of course, once they were sighted the keepers and police were out in force, and there was no way out, no way back down this glen, and so they were caught red-handed. So here was this gang of men, and a few lurchers, crossed collie-greyhounds, along with what they had been poaching – half a dozen white mountain hares. The really funny thing was, they didn't behave like you would expect poachers to: they didn't seem to be too much worried about the hares at all.

And then the story came out: what they were doing was organizing a live chase for betting on the dogs! They had come from the north of England, some of them from Scotland too, and they were taking the dogs to places where they knew there were mountain hares to be found. So they all walk up the mountain and as soon as a hare is flushed the dogs are loosed. It isn't really poaching, I suppose, because the main thing is betting on the dogs. They have a book down home and take a sort of guide and judge with them, and I believe that thousands and thousands of pounds are in the pot in bets. So you never know exactly what you are going to find on the hills, either causing bother or *in* some sort of bother.

The sheep are always finding trouble for themselves in poor weather, for example. If it comes on to snow, they will take shelter from the wind and will make for any wee cove of rock or the edge of a burn. And of course it doesn't take long for the snow to bury them. You have to be very quick to dig them out or they will be suffocated. It is not so long since I was helping a friend nearby and it was two or three weeks before we got all the sheep dug out. We were up there for days. Everyone was helping to dig them out, because it was a terrible storm. Eventually we did get all of them, but we were very lucky.

Or sheep can get carried away by an avalanche, just swept away, so I always try to feed my sheep close to sheltered and safe areas. We try very hard not to be caught out, but it does happen, so we like to think that we are on hand all the time to dig them out when necessary. Usually we just give them a bit of a whistle-up and they come running to their feeding time in the morning. You get a rough count then, and if there seems to be a lot absent, well, you just have to go and look for them and hope that they are OK.

And missing hill-walkers is something else we have to keep an eye open for. We like to make sure that when they go on the hill they know what they are doing and are equipped to survive if things turn nasty. You know – you could come across an empty tent somewhere in the glen, and you might not know where they were or what they were up to. Could there be a body lying in the snow somewhere, lying injured in a burn, or whatever?

You could say, well, it doesn't really have anything to do with us, but that's not the way the world works here. We live in the glen and know its moods, so we like to think that we can keep an eye on it at all times.

To tell the truth, hill-walkers have sometimes been a bit of a problem for some estates. Here in Glen Tilt, we have a right of way, which means that hill-walkers are allowed to travel the path through. But unfortunately a lot of people don't stick to the path; they think they have a roving commission. Now, that may well be so, but during our shooting season I think those people should give a wee bit more consideration to the people who have to do a job of work here.

I think some of the hill-walkers – not all of them, but to be sure some of them – have to think about us just that wee bit more. There's no problem with many of them, of course. Many

Notice to hill walkers

---

of them are very well prepared, very good at map-reading, and there is no problem with the genuine hill-man, or hill-woman, at all.

But the Munro-baggers aren't always like that – that's the folk who try to have been to the top of every hill in Scotland over 3000 feet. Some of them just like to zip up to the top and race back down again as quickly as possible and clock it off in their wee book, saying to themselves, 'That's another Munro that I have done'. Some of these people don't really seem to consider anyone else on the hill, be they working or stalking – or even other hill-walkers in some cases. So they are not the ideal people to have here at certain times of the year, because some of them – not all, mind – tend to have a different attitude to the mountains compared to the traditional hill-person.

On top of the grouse moor; a snow storm on the way

And the main reason they are not always ideal is because, often, they are just the sort of person to get into trouble. So my advice is that whenever they plan to go on the hill, they should be cautious above all else. They should phone up the landowner and just have a chat and ask if there is any work going on that day in the area they would like to walk in. They should ask if their presence there would disturb the work, and whether any alternative day would be suitable.

And when they finally do go to the hill, they should always leave a note to say where they are going, when they left, when they would hope to be back, what route they are taking, and that they are properly equipped to survive an emergency.

That means they should have a torch, a small pack of flares, clothing and food to cope with a dangerous situation. In other words they should have a thorough understanding of the countryside code as it relates to winter in the Scottish hills.

If there is an accident we call out the mountain rescue team at once; but we are often the first to get to the scene. And we have to be extremely careful when we get there, because obviously if someone has a suspected broken back – well, you must know what to do in that sort of circumstance. It is common sense not to try to move a dangerously injured person unless their life is at immediate risk from, say, an avalanche or whatever. We have carried people with broken legs off the hill before the mountain rescue team ever got near us, and have been swimming about in rivers pulling out people who have tumbled in and so on. So we feel that we are at least partly responsible for the people who come through the glen. After all, you can't leave someone on the hill, just sit at the fire and say, 'They should never have gone out anyway, and it's not my problem'.

That's just not the way things work here, whether it's giving another keeper or shepherd a hand in times of need, or rescuing climbers. And it's just as well that that's not the way things are, either. Because people are getting killed all too often on the Scottish hills in winter – not just on the highest hills, but all over, in any county. And as we are the first people who have to go out in Glen Tilt, then you can understand why we want to see trouble on the hills as little as possible.

DECEMBER

Of course, most of it is to blame on the weather – a lot of people just don't know what it can be like up here in really ferocious conditions. I suppose we see the first of the snow most years round about November, though it can be earlier or later. But usually you realize it's part of the furniture of the glen some time in November. You suddenly realize, without thinking too much about it at first, that on a quiet snowy morning you can see the tracks of all the animals that have been out and about the night before, whether otters, badgers or foxes. In fresh snow you can follow the trail of the fox, but if a blizzard comes on you know that he is lost for the meantime, because he is curled up somewhere with his tail over his snout and sound asleep.

And by December there is no end of snow to complicate things, whether it is work in the glen or simply getting up and down the road to Blair Atholl. But at least we know it can't last for ever, we know that the cold and the long, long nights can't go on for ever. Come the twenty-first or thereabouts, we arrive at the shortest day of the year – and the longest night. And then there's Christmas to celebrate, and New Year's Eve to follow. Maybe you'll know the old saying, 'one more, one less'? Well, that's just the way it is. That's life, whether for the birds and the beasts on the hill, or ourselves in the glen too, when it comes down to it. So once again, that's us into another year – and the life of the glen is ready to move on into it.

Further reading

There is a vast recreational, historical, political and ecological literature in the subject-area of Scottish deer-forestry. Though many of the best titles are out of print, they may be available in some libraries. The following list comprises sources notable for their readability, importance

JAMES BARRON, *The Northern Highlands in the Nineteenth Century*, three vols, 1907
Topical excerpts from the *Inverness Courier* which offer a good flavour of contemporary events

ISABELLA BEETON, *The Book of Household Management*, ninth ed., 1909
Than whom greater to introduce the wealthy wonders of the turn-of-the-century kitchen and shooting-lodge?

JOHN BUCHAN, *John Macnab*, 1925
A poaching romance set in the fictional estate of Crask. Buchan's usual narrative drive and lightness of touch (may) excuse his sexism, racism and shameless promotion of imperialism

ROBERT CRICHTON, *The Camerons*, 1973
All that Buchan is not, and just as well written: with its wonderful salmon-poaching sequence, far better so

FRANK FRASER DARLING, *A Herd of Red Deer*, 1937; *Natural History in the Highlands and Islands*, 1947
Great stuff by a great naturalist, who never overlooked the imperatives of human land-use either

MARGARET DODS, *The Cook and Housewife's Manual*, 1826
By a remarkable lady, and still very readable, not least for its section on game cookery

R. S. R. FITTER AND R. A. RICHARDSON, *Collins Pocket Guide to British Birds*, 1966
If for nothing else, it's marvellous for its pocket descriptions of bird-song and bird-sounds

G. E. FREEMAN AND F. H. SALVIN, *Falconry; with remarks on the training of otters and cormorants*, 1859
Practical research for the historian of fishing techniques on an international scale

PHILIP GASKELL, *Morvern Transformed*, 1968
An impeccably presented account of the transformation (some would say deformation) of a native community in the cause of deer-stalking

I. F. GRANT, *Highland Folk Ways*, 1961
Excellent stuff by someone who knew her subject (and many related ones) inside out

Further reading

AUGUSTUS GRIMBLE, *Deer Stalking*, 1886; *The Deer-forests of Scotland*, 1896
Memoir, advice and historical account (in some editions both titles are included in one volume). A classic in the league of SCROPE, but published half a century later

DUFF HART-DAVIS, *Monarchs of the Glen*, 1978
A modern, high-quality introduction to the history and sociology of deer-stalking in Scotland

JOHN HUMPHREYS, *Poachers' Tales*, 1991
Very readable, informative in a technical sense, and with a good, if short, bibliography

RICHARD JEFFERIES, *The Gamekeeper at Home*, 1878
An accurate if somewhat sobering taste of how things used to be, though mainly concerned with low-country gamekeeping

JOHN MCEWEN, *Who Owns Scotland?*, 1977
A lifetime-work which endeavours to update the 1874 register of Scottish estates in the context of a call for a Scottish Land Register: an essential if now somewhat dated work

JOHN MCGRATH, *The Cheviot, the Stag and the Black, Black Oil*, 1981
For a partisan and completely Highland view of the social consequences of unbridled sporting exploitation in the Scottish north, there is little better than the text of this stage and television play

OSGOOD MACKENZIE, *A Hundred Years in the Highlands*, 1921
A good introduction to Highland life in the nineteenth century, though concerned with the west coast

J. D. MACKIE, *A History of Scotland*, 1964
Elegant, witty and erudite in turn, and never improperly partisan. As good an introduction as any and a great deal better than most

CALUM MACLEAN, *The Highlands*, 1959
A little dated, and more of a memoir than a comprehensive survey, but still a wonderful introduction to the subject by a writer of unrivalled knowledge, understanding and sympathy

LEA MACNALLY, *Highland Year*, 1968; *Highland Deer Forest*, 1970; *The Year of the Red Deer*, 1975
All well-written and fairly recent introductions by a long-term professional gamekeeper

F. MARIAN MCNEILL, *The Scots Kitchen*, 1929
A great work of social history. Elegant, funny, passionate, profoundly informed – all this and recipes too! When will the kitchen, or the nation, see her likes again?

DANIEL MANNIX, *A Sporting Chance, Unusual Methods of Hunting*, 1968
A detailed survey of primitive and alternative hunting technologies, with an excellent bibliography. Strictly for the serious student of the subject

BRIAN P. MARTIN, *Tales of the Old Gamekeepers*, 1989
Based largely on the experiences of low-country gamekeepers, but packed with useful information and illustrations

MAIRTIN O MURCHU, *East Perthshire Gaelic*, Dublin Institute for Advanced Studies, 1989
For anyone who wonders why so many of the place-names of Atholl

appear to be in a language other than
English

WILLIE ORR, *Deer Forests,
Landlords and Crofters*, 1982
An excellent academic work by a
former hill-shepherd. Though it
concentrates on counties to the
north of Perthshire, it is the
standard history, and deservedly so

S. POPE, *Hunting with Bow and
Arrow*, 1925
One for historians of pre-
gunpowder hunting methods

JAMES RITCHIE, *The Influence of
Man on Animal Life in Scotland*,
1920
A sobering account of destruction
and devastation by a writer many
years ahead of his time

WILLIAM SCROPE, *The Art of Deer
Stalking*, 1839
Primarily a classic memoir and dated
stylistically, but enormously
influential in encouraging the
growth of deer-stalking

W. M. SMITH, *The Romance of
Poaching in the Highlands*, 1904
Readable, and one of the very few
titles (if not the only one) to tell the
poacher's side of the story

ROBERT SOMERS, *Letters from
the Highlands*, 1848
A key polemical text with a
number of chapters concentrating
on the Forest of Atholl and
Glen Tilt

JOHN SOBIESKI STUART AND
CHARLES EDWARD STUART, *Lays
of the Deer Forest*, two vols, 1848
The second volume is much the best,
with a lot of still-relevant
information on the craft and art of
stalking

A. S. WALKER AND P. J. MACKIE,
The Keeper's Book, 1904
A guide to the duties of a
gamekeeper from the early years of
this century

MICHAEL WIGAN, *The Scottish
Highland Estate*, 1991; *Stag at Bay*,
1993
Both excellent works which make a
persuasive case, at least under
certain circumstances, for the
well-managed sporting estate
of today

WALTER WINANS, *The Sporting
Rifle*, 1908
By a master shot who took his sport
very seriously indeed. In many ways
a classic of shooting literature